What Others Are Saying
About this Book

"Spellbinding! Hard to put down; a twist at every corner!" — **Ray Arco, Hollywood Foreign Press Association, and voting member of the Golden Globes**

"Memoirs are special because they showcase legacy. *IRON BLOOD* is special in that is it preserves history. A really special book." — **Aura Imbarus, Ph.D., author,** *Out of the Transylvania Night*

"*IRON BLOOD* is a compelling, historical memoir of culture and tradition that seeks to find answers, unleashing three hundred years of intrigue in the process. A story of deep faith and hope." — **The V. Rev. Fr. Constantin Alecse, Sr. Pastor Holy Trinity Romanian Orthodox Church, Los Angeles**

"*IRON BLOOD: 300 Years of the Dmitri Kantemir Dynasty* exposes readers to an epic time from the past where so much went untold — until now. The author, a descendant of Dmitri Kantemir, Princess (Her Serene Highness) Eleonora Borisovna Kantemir, takes us on a journey exposing centuries of history, secrets and royal — and not so royal — shenanigans. Enjoy this story — perfect for a mini-series rivaling the likes of *Poldark* or *Downton Abby*." — **Lindy Hudis, author of Crashers, and, Producer — Impact Motion Pictures**

"From the Ottoman Empire to the charms of Moldavia, to life and times of Czarist Russia, this is a magical book of cultural traditions that entices the lovers of history to learn more." — **Ron Russell, author of** *Don Carina: World War II Mafia Herione*

"*IRON BLOOD* is a bold story showcasing the richness of historical events." —**Gary Chafetz, twice nominated for a Pulitzer-Prize by the Boston Globe, and, author of** *The Search for the Lost Army: The National Geographic and Harvard University Expedition*

"A touching story that brings the past into the present to make sense of the future." —**Marina Giurescu, author of** *A World Torn Asunder: The Life & Triumph of Constantin C. Giurescu*

IRON BLOOD
300 Years of the Dmitri Kantemir Dynasty

Princess (Her Serene Highness) Eleonora Borisovna Kantemir

An Imprint of Bettie Youngs Books
www.BettieYoungsBooks.com

Disclaimer: This is a true story, and the characters and events are real. However, in some cases the names, descriptions, and locations have been changed, and some events have been altered, combined, or condensed for storytelling purposes, but the overall chronology is an accurate depiction of the author's experience. The images used within this book are from Wikipedia and believed to be in the public domain.

The cover photo is a portrait of Ekaterina Dmitrievna Kantemir (daughter of Dmitri Kantemir) by Louis Michel Van Loo (1759). The painting is now displayed at the Pushkin Museum of Fine Arts in Moscow, Russia.

Cover Design by Tatomir Pitariu
Text Design by Jane Hagaman
Bettie Youngs Book Publishers / Burres Books—an Imprint of Bettie Youngs Books
www.BettieYoungsBooks.com

If you are unable to order this book from your local bookseller, or from wholesalers *Baker&Taylor* or *Ingram*, or online from *Amazon* or *Barnes & Noble*, or from *Espresso*, or *Read How You Want* (Large Print, Braille, Daisy), you may order directly from the publisher: sales@BettieYoungsBooks.com

Trade Paperback: ISBN: 978-1-940784-51-9
eBook: 978-1-940784-52-6
Hardback: 978-1-940784-58-8

Library of Congress Control Number available upon request.
1. Literary collections: Eastern Europe; Russia; former Soviet States—1688-present. 2. Historical Memoirs. 3. Culture of Ottoman Empire. 4. St. Petersburg. 5. Life at Tsaritsyno Estate. 6. Prince Dmitri Kantemir. 7. Battle of the Pruth in Moldavia. 8. Displaced Persons after World War II. 9. HSH Eleonora Borisovna Kantemir. 10. Ella Kantemir. 11. Ray Arco. 12. Hollywood Foreign Press Association. 13. The Golden Globes. 14. Czarist Russia. 15. Moldavia. 16. Azerbaijan. 17. Princess Eleonora Borisovna Kantemir.

This book is dedicated to:

MY CHILDREN:
Paul Wollman Jr.
Altynai and Alexa Fung

And in memory of
Dina Karanowytsch

Table of Contents

Acknowledgments

Collaboration and Consultants:

Bettie Youngs, of Bettie Youngs Book Publishing and Burres Books

Ray Arco, *Principal Collaborator:* West Hollywood, California

Ileana Matac Arco: West Hollywood, California

Lydia King: London England

Mona Moore: Santa Monica, California

Ferit F. Kayrak: Istanbul, Turkey

Pat and Ron Tildage: Los Angeles, California

Ricky Tsai: Los Angeles, California

Eileen Au: Los Angeles, California

Cindy Yang: Los Angeles, California

Allen Lee: Los Angeles, California

Special Thanks

I would like to express my sincere thanks to my mentor, my guiding light and dear friend, Ray Arco. Without him this story would have remained in the past.

My utmost gratitude goes to Bettie Youngs of Bettie Youngs Book Publishing Co. for her diligence and professional guidance in bringing this book to print. Her belief in me and her guidance in telling this story made this book possible: I forever remain in her debt.

I extend my deepest appreciation to Mona Moore—where a chance meeting on a train led to an Alpha sister who offered unconditional guidance in writing this book.

My sincere appreciation to my life-long friend, Lydia King, who put up with my endless escapades in researching London's history for this book.

My special thanks go out to Joan Winter for her encouraging words and for accompanying me on this literary journey.

With special words of love to my sister, Ella: *"Dreams do come true."*

AND

Betty Blair, editor and founder of Azerbaijan International Magazine.

Olivia at Serbianna at Serbianna.com.

Tiberiu Pintillie, administrator, "Romanianmonasteries.org."

Introduction

I am a descendant of the Dmitri Kantemir dynasty. Prince Dmitri Kantemir (1673—1723), Prince of Moldavia, Prince of the Russian Empire, Prince of the Holy Roman Empire and Imperial Chancellor to Peter the Great of Russia, lived in forced exile for 22 years in Istanbul. He became a great writer, statesman, scientist, composer of Ottoman music and a great linguist speaking and writing in eleven languages. His talents passed to his children, who were prominent in Russian history. His son, Antioch Kantemir was Russia's first satirist and Russia's Ambassador to England and France. His elder daughter Maria toured Europe as an accomplished virtuoso harpsichordist. Notably, she was the last love of Russia's Czar, Peter the Great.

Obviously that period of time is long, long ago. Centuries even. The Kantemir story was all but forgotten in the shadows of time—until the family of Boris Karanowytsch (my father) found their way to America in 1952.

As a child, a good number of things about my legacy were revealed to me, but it only whetted my appetite to know more. The older I got, the more curious I became. I wanted to know more about lives of the Kantemirs, their historical accomplishments and contributions. Who were they in everyday life, and what were their lives like? Above all, I thirsted for answers as to stories of deception regarding our family and associated with us, and concerning my growing suspicions surrounding the circumstances my father's death. And I wondered why mysterious, unexplained events still followed the living descendants of the Kantemir dynasty—me included—into the twenty-first century.

During the research for this book, I learned more of my ancestry and heritage. I discovered that portions of the Kantemir estate, namely a palace in St. Petersburg and a smaller one in Istanbul, had been confiscated. I learned that a 1685 Ewer & Basin heirloom was taken and unlawfully sold by the Soviets, and is now housed at the Metropolitan Museum of Art in New York. And I discovered the reason why my father was hunted by the KGB—and why the Kantemir's were the target of Soviet intelligence operatives.

Aside from missing castles, art, jewels and land, I discovered that I had a living sister who shared my same name—and, that my own true identity is that of a Princess. I am *"Her Serene Highness Eleonora Borisovna Kantemir."*

But what other secrets and surprises did the Kantemir dynasty harbor? This is my story.

—Princess Eleonora Borisovna Kantemir,
Fall 2015

1

A New Beginning — From Germany, to America

Karlsruhe, Germany—1951. World War II had ended seven years earlier. The town was in the process of rebuilding itself, as was all of Germany. Remnants of ruins among the newly restored buildings were the only reminders of a global war, responsible for the deadliest conflict in human history.

As a four year-old, I was unaware of all of that. I was engrossed in my own world of childhood activities. My life in Germany was good and one of privilege. Our family had a housekeeper and a nanny and I wore the best clothes and attended a private school. I was learning to speak German. Although, I was born in Germany, I was just learning to speak the language, as Russian was the primary language spoken in our household. Both of my parents were from Russia. During

World War II the Nazi's took my mother as slave labor. Papa, as I called my father, had managed to escape from the communists during the turmoil of the battle.

A daily outing with mother at the local park in Karlsruhe was my favorite past time. Today was no exception. I walked hand in hand with mother to the park's grounds that were covered with sprouting yellow and white daises. My wish of the moment was to pick as many daises as I could to fill my small wicker basket. I was determined to pack the flowers to the very top and impress mother. I couldn't wait to get started as we neared the park. I dropped my mother's hand, running ahead to a white patch of flowers. Stooping down, almost feverishly, I began to pick as many daises as I could, ever so often glancing back at mother to make sure that in the excitement I hadn't drifted off too far. My basket was almost full when mother cried out.

"Ella, Ella, come here. I'm going to braid some of those daises in your hair."

I turned to see mother waving at me from underneath a shaded tree. I wanted those daises in my hair, to feel more special than I already felt. I ran to mother as fast as I could and by the time I reached her I was panting and out of breath. Falling on a red-checkered blanket that was sprawled on the grass, I threw the wicker basket alongside. Mother didn't waste any time. She took a daisy from my basket and began weaving it into a braid on the top of my head until it was entirely covered with the delicate, miniature daisies. Outlining the daisy tiara with my hand, the effect pleased me.

"Stay right there, don't move. I'm going to take your photograph," said mother.

I must look extraordinary, I thought feeling ever so enchanted. I immediately stood up to straighten my white polka-dotted dress and adjusted my matching wide brimmed hat to make sure that my blond bangs were visible. That hat had to be positioned several times before I got it just right. For some unknown reason everything had to be perfect and that was the way it was with me. I always had to look and be at my best.

"You look beautiful. I shall take a few more photographs which will be ready in a few days," said mother.

A week later, when I arrived home from kindergarten, I saw mother looking at a few photographs displayed on the table.

"Come take a look," she said.

I ran to the table and began to scrutinize the photographs carefully. To my disappointment, the hat completely concealed the flowers in my hair. In the fuss to position the hat just right to ensure my bangs were visible, I had forgotten about the beautiful crown of daises atop my head. *I will have to be more careful next time. Anything of importance should be visible. This shall not occur again,* was the mental note I made.

A watch gifted by my father was my first piece of jewelry. The timepiece with its wide brown leather band practically covered my entire wrist. I wore it proudly and made sure to display it whenever the opportunity arose. When told there was to be a family photograph session I immediately knew that I would be wearing my favorite piece of jewelry, and that it had to be visible in the photograph. I decided to wear my white cashmere sweater, the one with the round collar that would complement the watch. The sweater with its crystal like buttons sparkled whenever the light hit them at a certain angle. A beige dress beneath would complete the ensemble, '*There now, I am fit as a princess should be for an official photography,*' I thought to myself, impressed with my fashion choice.

"We're ready with the lighting," said the photographer. "Everyone take their places, please."

I took my place next to mother, a diminutive woman that commanded an air of authority for when she spoke, everyone listened. Even papa dared not say a word. This was probably due to the fact of what mother endured when taken from her homeland as an eleven-year-old child as forced labor by the Nazi's. She was pushed, shoved, and herded onto freight trains, along with other women, men and crying children. The trains headed for Poland with only cracks in the wood allowing clean air to enter. There was no room for privacy, only room for lost dignity, and eventually lost lives as prisoners of war. Once there, the women and children were separated from the men. They were told to undress and to take a shower. My mother was the last one in line and when the shower door opened she heard a woman holding a baby scream out, "What did we do to deserve this?"

Just as quickly, everyone was shoved through the door; it closed right in front of my mother. She was spared, saved by a female Nazi officer who in fact was secretly attempting to save as many prisoners from the gas chambers as she could. It turned out that his beautiful officer, who wore her blonde hair in one long braid that hung down her back, was married to a German commander.

"Quickly, get dressed! I am going to revise your papers to show that you are half German," she said in fluent Russian to my mother.

My mother was further surprised to learn that this amazing officer was a Russian citizen who risked her life to save as many people as she could by forging their documents. Consequently, she arranged for my mother to be adopted by a childless German couple.

Yes, mother was tough and even more so a survivor. Throughout all the adversity, she still managed to develop a high sense of fashion. It was mother who made sure everyone was presentable when going out. She was always stylishly dressed and her flair for fashion must have influenced me, for I always had to look "just right." Mother's most repeated words,

"*Do not embarrass your selves when you go* out" still rings in my ears. When people stopped and admired my look, I was satisfied as I knew I didn't disappoint mother and most importantly, I hadn't embarrassed myself.

Papa stood alongside me to my right. He looked very distinguished, even handsome in his dark blue suit. I felt he was very important. He was extraordinary in my eyes. Everything was more interesting when papa was around. I felt he had a keen insight when it came to life and his observations, although I didn't know it at the time, proved to be correct. Curious and mysterious situations that arose throughout my life were to confirm that.

"One, two, three smile." The photographer interrupted any further thoughts about papa. As if on cue, I quickly lifted the sleeve of my sweater, it was just enough for the watch to be seen. I learned from the *daisies* incident and did not want a repeat. My important watch needed to be visible. A quick flash of light from the camera followed and I was confident that this time the results would be pleasing.

It was not until a few months later that my life was to take a dramatic change. It startled me right out of a deep sound sleep.

"Hurry, time to get up," called my mother.

Time to get up, what was mother talking about? It was still very dark outside. Why was mother scrambling about? What was going on? It was cold and I did not want to get out of my comfortable warm bed. I glanced at the window and I could see it was snowing outside.

"Hurry, get out of bed," repeated mother.

I had no choice, but to listen to mother and get out of bed. I had to dress quickly. My eyes were trying to adjust to the bright light in the room. The hustle and bustle was confusing—however, I dared not ask any questions. I hurriedly put on my white fur collared wool coat.

The entire family hustled down the stairs and into a waiting car filled with suitcases. Why were they in a hurry? Where were they going? What was happening? Before, I could think or comprehend anything in my sleepy state; I was on an airplane and leaving Germany. I did not know where we were going or what was to happen. All I knew was that I was leaving my wonderful secure life in Germany. I looked out the airplane window. It was still very dark. A bright yellow crescent moon lit up the black sky and an endless road of shinning stars guided the way. The constant hum of propellers soon lulled me to sleep. Little did I realize that my privileged life was not only unraveling, but would come to a complete stop. I was about to enter a new life, a foreign life. My once simple existence would get more complicated, for not only would I have to learn to adapt to a new life; that life would also expose the many secrets that surrounded my family.

AMERICA—February, 1952. I clutched my doll tightly as I walked down the stairwell of the "Flying Tiger" airplane at Idlewild Airport in New York. My entire family made their way into the terminal and to the end of a line where a uniformed man was speaking a language I have never heard. When it was our turn, I could see stamping and turning of pages at the counter where the uniformed man stood. In familiar German, I heard, *"Oh! That is the Karanowytsch family. They are displaced persons, refugees. Take their fingerprints and photographs."*

That sentence and the manner of the uniformed man made me feel very uneasy. What a strange place and now they wanted our individual photographs to be taken. I did not like it at all. Why were we being called these strange names? This new place was not nice and from what I had observed in this short time, the people seemed uncivilized. Was this a correct decision, to come to this new place? Father said America would provide greater opportunities, a better life.

What were my parents thinking, a new life a better life? I could not understand or make sense of it. We became known as "DP'S", short for displaced persons. That's what we were called by the people in this new land. No one was respected. Didn't they know whom they were speaking to? I was not accustomed to what I saw or heard and was made fun of. Some told me to *"go back where you came from."* Many times I wished I could have. I wanted to get back on the airplane and return to Germany. Unfortunately, I had no choice. I had to accept this alien life that was forced upon me.

I looked about the small two-room house where my family now lived. It certainly was not better. It was a far cry from our comfortable life in Karlsruhe. I shared sleeping quarters with my siblings that doubled as a living room. My parents slept in a room that was part of a kitchen. A communal bathroom with only a toilet was located in the hallway and shared with neighbors. On Saturday nights, mother would heat water on the stove and pour it in a big steel tub in the middle of the kitchen. Everyone took turns to bathe. Clothing and my first pair of new shoes was purchased from thrift stores. What has happened to my family and me! Money did not grow on trees as was rumored in Germany. Suddenly, reality set in.

A princess does not live like this. Whatever gave me such an idea! For the first time I was embarrassed by the notion. In this country I was not even a normal being. I felt sorry for myself and for my family. Life would not be easy. We were not welcomed in this country. We were intruding where we were not wanted. Being stateless, we were citizens of nowhere. To make it more difficult, no one in the family spoke English. We had to learn from one another, which probably explains the reason why to this day I speak English with an unusual accent. I had difficulty pronouncing words starting with "*th*." The word *chalk* was confused with *eraser*. Everyone at school laughed at me. Why did everyone hate me so? What did I do to them? I tried so hard to fit in.

I stopped wearing my hair in my favorite style—braids. I thought, after that, I looked like everyone else with my blond hair and green eyes, but somehow I was still different. Everything about me was different, my mannerism, my thinking and my looks. I could not be one of them no matter how hard I tried. I simply did not fit in. I became painfully aware that I would have to fend for myself in this new country.

It was mother, who was familiar with harsh conditions that had the perfect antidote. I was enrolled in ballet classes. Dance, a channel to express and release feelings, became a way to communicate through grace and style that not even poetic words could express. It became my new friend. Dance would allow me to excel and ignore all the negativity that I faced from this new country. I would dance through this alien life with grace and patience. My new life was going to be a ballet!

2

Two Sisters —

with the Same Name

New Britain, Connecticut — 1953. Today seemed no different than any other as I arrived home from school. Even though I was six years old and felt grown up, I still enjoyed my childhood games. I had enough time to play in the backyard before I needed to start my homework. The afternoon sun warmed my shoulders as I ran down the steps of the back porch and out into the huge hilly yard. I loved to sit in the yard, on top of the slope that overlooked the town and the Fafnir Bearing Company where papa worked. Sometimes, I could see him at the second floor factory window, waving at me with a white handkerchief and I would wave back. Today, to my disappointment, I did not see papa at the window.

This caused me to run to the top of the sloop, looking up

at the factory window and no matter how and where I looked I could not see papa. Finally, I noticed him at the end of the long narrow yard. He was sitting on an old, worn out stuffed chair. His hand, resting on the exposed dirty cushion, held a large envelope with a strange stamp affixed in the upper right corner. I wondered why papa was home so early from work. I ran down to greet him.

"Papa, Papa! What are you doing, just sitting there?" I yelled.

Papa looked up at me, his eyes wet with tears. I walked to a nearby rock and sat down, hugging my arms around my knees, as I gazed up at him.

"Papa, what is the matter?" I asked.

"I received a letter from the Soviet Union. It contains bad news," he replied.

"What kind of bad news, papa?" I asked looking at the paper in his hand.

"My cousin's letter says your grandmother, my mother, had died."

"I'm so sorry that I never got to know her. When did it happen?" I further inquired.

"Ten years ago," said papa with tears streaming down his cheeks.

"Why didn't your cousin tell you sooner?" I asked.

"Ellatchka, recently my cousin received the news that your grandmother died in Siberia, in the labor camps where criminals and political prisoners were held. The conditions of these labor camps were very harsh and she was exiled there. The government sent her to the gulags because of me and it's entirely my fault and I am responsible," he continued as he covered his face with his hands and sobbed.

I could feel papa's anguish. He was in agony about a decision he had made decades ago, but why was he responsible?

What kind of decision would cause papa to suffer so? Being an inquisitive child, I was determined to learn more.

"Why would anyone send a harmless old woman to Siberia? You once told me she was a nurse on the Russian front. She put her own life in danger to care for wounded soldiers. I don't understand."

"There is more to it than that, my little one. There is a lot you don't know, but I shall tell you something of significance in my life that may also affect yours. When I was a young child in Russian, I witnessed my father being shot by the Bolsheviks. They took power in Russia in 1917 during the Russian Revolution. That day is still imprinted in my mind as if it happened yesterday. I shall never forget it! I was walking with my father to the railroad station where he worked. Once we arrived, we were ambushed. The Bolsheviks ran out from behind the trees, called us enemy of the people and aimed their rifles at my father. He fell to the ground and I knew he was dead. I ran as fast as I could to get away. I ran and ran and dared not look back. They did not find me, but I knew I would be next. For many years after, I was cautious, just waiting to be eradicated—my crime, being a descendant of nobility and an enemy of the new communist government. I never had an opportunity to do anything about it. When World War II broke out, I took the opportunity and fled Russia as not to suffer the same fate as my father. I eventually was taken prisoner by the Germans. I was doing forced roadwork for them when shrapnel hit me in my arm, causing it to be amputated. After that, I had no choice but to do what I did. I became a volunteer in the fight against the communists."

"Papa, but why was grandmother sent to Siberia? Was it your fight against the communists, or was it your escape from the Soviet Union?" I looked at papa's expressionless face. His eyes seemed to be avoiding me. "Is there something else you are not telling me?"

Two Sisters—with the Same Name | 11

"The conditions for prisoners of war were inhuman and horrendous and I was tormented by the choice of either perishing behind barbed wire in a labor camp or betraying my own people by serving the Germans," he answered. "Eventually, I gave in. I detested the communists and being a member of the nobility further complicated matters. I felt there was no hope and without hope there is no future. I had no alternative but to commit a crime against the Soviet government. I joined the Russian Liberation Movement."

Papa remained silent for a few moments. He could scarcely bear to look at me.

"I knew I could never return to the Soviet Union, since I would be executed. That's what Stalin did to prisoners of war—killed them or sent them into exile. The Bolsheviks could not find me. It did not occur to me that they would arrest Maria Kolasova, your grandmother. She was sent to Siberia for what I did. My escape and actions in Germany were crimes against the state. It is all my doing. I am the one responsible."

"Papa, are the Soviets still looking for you?" I asked. I could see he was deep in thought.

After a few moments of silence he answered.

"It is worse. When you are older, I shall tell you more about the Russian Liberation Movement and my involvement."

I looked at papa and thought, *Papa, poor Papa. He has been carrying the guilt of what he did in silence for decades.* I got up and gave him a big hug; unable to say anything that would make him feel better. I knew he loved his mother very much. The turn of the century photograph of a beautiful young blonde lady in a nurse's uniform had been displayed on the family table for as long as I could remember.

"Ella, that is not all. I left something else behind in the Soviet Union," continued papa. He took a tattered photograph from his shirt pocket. "This is your sister."

I looked at the worn photograph, a picture of a blonde toddler with uneven cut bangs across her forehead and a bandanna around her neck. We eerily looked similar.

"I cut her bangs myself and put that bandanna around her neck for the photograph," papa said proudly.

I was not shocked or surprised by this new revelation. I was proud that papa thought I was grown up enough to understand such complicated things in life. I wanted to learn all there was about my newly found sister.

"Papa, how old is she?" I brought my knees to my chin, hugging them tighter as I waited for his answer.

"She is nine years older than you. She is fifteen years old now," replied father.

"I have a teenage sister in Russia!" I exclaimed excitedly. "What is her name?"

"You and her share the same name, *Eleonora Borisovna*," was the reply.

"So, there are two of us, Papa?"

"Yes, you were named after your sister," he said as he returned the photograph to his shirt pocket. "I always carry this picture with me, here in my left shirt pocket, close to my heart."

Those words drew me closer to a sister I had never met. I felt guilty, knowing I was growing up with a father and she was not. I wondered, did my sister know she had a sibling on the opposite side of the world—in America?

"Maybe, one day we shall find her and then we all can be happy together," I said with the innocence of a child. I got up from my place on the rock, walked over to papa and put my hands on his shoulders to show my support.

A slight smile of hope crept across papa's face, which was then quickly shadowed by sadness.

"I cannot return. The hands of time can never be reversed. I will be killed."

"Papa, does that mean I am in danger, too?" I asked without quite realizing what I was questioning.

His unexpected response frightened me: "No! They only want ME!"

3

A Russian Scout Camp — Summer 1963

Established in 1687, the town of New Britain, Connecticut was situated among landscapes of rolling hills, woods, and many parks. Umbrella trees with their enormous spectrum of khaki foliage lined the town's streets, shading the rays of a hot summer sun. Tomatoes, cucumbers and an array of vegetables grew in between vibrant rows of the many flowerbeds that dominated the front lawn of every home. Located above the homes, was the emerald knoll of Walnut Hill Park. Colorful assortments of blooming rose gardens were scattered on the slope of the hill. They were a miniature paradise for the young to run through, dodging the prickly thorns as they made their way to the enormous circular water pond featuring a small fountain in the center, the crown of Walnut Hill Park. Children waded in the pond during the summers, their faces cooled off by the sprays of the fountain. On the perimeter of the park was a nut shaped alabaster shell where orchestras played during special events. Many motley blankets covered the grassy slopes as locals listened to the rhythm of the orchestra playing to the vibration of spectacular fireworks during 4th of July celebrations.

In the early 60's, Walnut Hill Park was at the top of the world. The park's white gazebos of old fashioned wooden benches was the perfect place to sit and admire the scenic view of the township. New Britain, with its turn of the century houses, was at the base, curtsying to the guests as they left the park. The grand finale was a miniature round kiosk, its small iceboxes filled with twenty five cent ice-cream sandwiches and cones, bidding the guests farewell as they enjoyed their treat. Around the corner, in a gray-stoned historical building, was the town post office. It was constructed at the turn of the 20th century. Its ashen marble interior walls contrasted with its dark, polished, wood floors. Clerks at numerous small arched windows took packages and sold 3-cent stamps. In the corner, a small newsstand sold magazines, newspapers, and candy. A ritual for many residents was to stop in daily and pick up the *New Britain Herald* or the *New York Daily News*, even if not purchasing stamps or sending parcels.

Across the street from the post office, two early 1900's gray-stoned public libraries sat side by side. The larger one with huge windows, contained floor to ceiling shelves of endless books. There were rows of tables for those doing research or homework. The smaller building next door was for younger children and contained a small museum on the lower level. On the way down and on the left wall of the staircase, a glass exhibition of an ant colony was displayed. Thousands of insects scurried through their many sand tunnels. It was an amazing sight. Where were they going? What were they doing scrambling about so? Building more tunnels? Did they have any thoughts, these amazing beings with architectural genius? At the bottom of the staircase, a room containing small preserved animals and an enclosed glass display of mice, gerbils and other small wonders of nature greeted the children. Both libraries had mammoth unused fireplaces.

The fear of a fantasy, of a wicked witch stirring her mystical brew of mice tails and rat's eyes, while a hovering black cat lurked nearby, just waiting for the right opportunity to snap at an early meal, was a powerful determent to keep children at bay and away from the fireplace.

Further down the road, was Capital Luncheonette. It was the place to go on Friday night where the townspeople sat at its long counter enjoying the specialty of the house—long hot dogs piled high with homemade sauerkraut. Afterwards, a stroll down Main Street or a movie at the grandiose Strand Theater, with its enormous crystal chandelier hanging precariously from the center of the towering ceiling, would conclude a simple, but gratifying evening before heading home along Broad Street, the neighborhood of the largest Polish community in Connecticut. Banks, businesses, bakeries and little shops dominated the area where English was rarely spoken or heard. Nearby was Sacred Heart Church and its school where nuns dressed in black habits, with rosaries dangling from their waists, taught the students.

New Britain was a significant manufacturing center, the *"Hardware Capital of the World,"* home to Stanley Works, Corbin Locks and the Fafnir Bearing Company. This was the town that my family settled in when we first arrived in 1952 from Germany.

Our home was at 34 Orange Street, just across from Sacred Heart. Although, I did not attend the school, I liked to look across the street and observe each day's activities because the play area was always noisy and vibrant where children enjoyed their games of hopscotch and jump rope. As I entered my teenage years in the small town, I did not think too much about my newly discovered sister.

It was the 60's, an age of evolution and revolution, a time of change, conflict and new ideas. America was a young country with nearly half of its population under eighteen years of age and no one over forty was to be trusted. College and university students believed in freedom of speech. Peaceful sit-ins and demonstrations were held against the war in Vietnam and draft dodgers fled to Canada to avoid service in the military. Love and peace were the words of this generation. Martin Luther King spread inspirational words of peace and against hatred. Communism, capitalism, the cold war, nuclear power, and the space race with the U.S.S.R. all brought the sixties to new heights.

The Cuban Missile Crisis almost brought the world to nuclear war during the term of the 35th president of America — John F. Kennedy. American troops were ready to invade Cuba and the Soviet Union was ready to attack the U.S. It was a time of awakening.

As an adolescent of the sixties, I yearned for adventure and new discoveries. When my parents decided to send me and my siblings off to a camp for children of Russian immigrants I excitedly counted the days. The entire summer would be spent in Jackson, New Jersey, with others of our ethnicity, many who had hidden noble origins. Papa mentioned that we too had noble lineage. I eagerly looked forward to all the new friends I would make and to the two months I would be there. I knew this time I would fit in and I was tired of listening to all the turmoil of world events with nothing good going on. A getaway at a secluded camp in the countryside would allow me to put the havoc of current events out of my thoughts. Quietness would be a welcome relief alongside an opportunity to learn more of my cultural background, much of which seemed secret lately.

I noticed papa was acting strangely, almost frightened at times. Could his recently revived correspondence with an old friend, Nicholas, have anything to do with his guarded behavior? I did not have the courage to ask, or perhaps, I did not want to know. I knew he was reluctant to discuss anything to do with the past—his past. There was much to do, so I decided not to dwell on papa's peculiar behavior any longer.

I neatly folded several navy blue skirts and navy blue shorts and placed them in a small green Samsonite suitcase on the bed. Uniforms were the norm for the scout camp I would be attending. A khaki style military shirt to be worn daily would be given to me when I arrived.

I listened to Shelley Fabrare's hit song, *Johnny Angel*, on my transistor radio, my best friend. I often placed it to my ear when static would interrupt my favorite songs. I took it everywhere I went, but I would not this time. The camp did now allow the modern luxuries of the 20th century. It would only *spoil the mind*, thought the elders from the old country. Rock and roll music would have to be forfeited for the summer. The songs of the Beach Boys' hit *Surfin,* or *Twisting* with Chubby Checkers, as well as the hits of the Four Seasons would have to wait until my return home.

I only had a few minutes left to finalize my packing. My family was waiting for me by the curbside. I quickly closed my suitcase and walked over to the mirror to check my dress and makeup. I needed some lipstick. *Tutti Fruity* was the name of my favorite shade and I would wear it today. I applied the pale pink lipstick and reached over to the dresser for a tissue. I blotted my lips with it, so the lipstick would last longer. Now, it was

A Russian Scout Camp—Summer 1963 | 19

time to work on my hair, a feat in itself. The front was short and the back very long. I teased and sprayed the front of my blonde hair into a nice bouffant, the higher the better. I gathered the long part of my hair into a high ponytail that hung to the middle of my back. I sprayed my hair again. *One can never have enough hairspray,* I thought as I threw the can of spray into the suitcase. I went through one can a week to hold my trademark style, which I had copied from actress Connie Stevens, whom I admired and wanted to emulate. Her picture, alongside that of Troy Donahue's was posted on my bedroom wall. Hollywood was a far cry from the small Connecticut town where I lived, but with perseverance I felt that I could also accomplish what was important to me, just like Connie and Troy. They were successful and I knew they must have come from small towns, too. Perseverance was the key to any endeavor. *"Good-bye Connecticut, hello New Jersey,"* I said aloud to no one in particular as the car left the curb for the three-hour ride.

Camp P.O.R.R. was an acronym for *Patriarch Organization of Russian Scouts.* It was situated in the back woods, far off a main road. Its many green acres of abundant shady trees, a volleyball court and endless activities enabled the scouts to share and experience their beliefs and customs. Young people were helped to adjust to a new life in a new country and at the same time allowed to continue learning about the old ways of their mother country left behind. Volleyball and ping-pong were a few of the many afternoon activities, following a morning of study that included writing, reading, history and poetry.

A week passed and I had settled comfortably into the routine of the camp. The air was fresh with the scent of crisp green trees. I took a deep breath as I walked to the study area. I loved the aroma of the morning dew on the grass, which seemed similar to apples. I was scheduled to attend a class in Russian history and because it was such a beautiful sunny day I would have preferred not to be there, listening to what was probably a boring subject, with all its Czars and Czarinas, most related, all with the same names, wagering various wars—same circumstances, different characters. *However, the subject today was going to be Peter the Great who had developed St. Petersburg and had the reputation of being the greatest Czar of all Russia. It might be interesting after all,* I thought,

I glanced around the many rows of tables. The outdoor classroom was almost filled to capacity. 'Hmm,' I thought as I turned to my left. To my surprise, papa was taking a seat next to me. "Papa, what are you doing here? This is a class for students."

"The professor doesn't mind. He welcomes the attention. He is a noted authority on Russian history. Look behind me. I am not the only one interested in old Russia. They are eagerly anticipating the commencement of today's lesson, as am I," he casually remarked.

A group of elderly men, with enthusiastic expressions sat behind us. All conversation came to a halt as a robust professor made his way to a board set up in front of the classroom where a large map hung.

"Let us start immediately!" he exclaimed excitedly.

He picked up a cue stick from a nearby desk and began his narrative: "Peter the Great! We are all aware of his many great contributions, talents and numerous battles for a greater Russia. We shall be discussing one of his many battles, but it will not be a victory battle we shall talk about today. The battle we shall be discussing is the *Battle of the Prut*, which was against the Ottoman Turks. They controlled Moldavia and Wallachia."

The professor continued waving his cue stick about until it stopped on a designated area on the map. He spoke with authority, loudly proclaiming information in a deep voice, as if he were Peter the Great himself. "Here is Moldavia on the north and Wallachia to the south. Moldavia was a country full of green forests and lush hills. Iasi, the center of Moldavian activity, was a picturesque city of uplands and woods, partly on two hills and partly between valleys. Although, the country was situated among vineyards and gardens the name was derived from the Moldova River. Dmitri Cantemir, Prince of Moldavia, writes about the country in detail in his *Descriptio Moldaviae*. According to the story, the ruler of the time, Dragos, took his hound, Molda, on a hunting trip for aurochs: large wild cattle. Molda spotted an auroch, but when she approached the animal, she was attacked and killed on the shores of an unknown nearby river. Dragos, devastated by the loss of his favorite hound, named the river after her.

"There are many churches and monasteries scattered throughout the country. The Church of the *Three Hierachs* was built in 1637. Intricate interwoven embroidery designs of stone laced the upper walls of the church. The church established not only the spirituality of the people, but also the culture of Moldavia. Prince Dmitri of Moldavia, his wife Cassandra Cantacuzenes and their six children often attended vespers and holy liturgy there. Pay attention and focus. We are going to move forward to another geographic location," continued the professor, as he waved his cue stick about. *What a silly looking man; who knew that someone so strange would have so much knowledge?* I thought.

"This is Istanbul, Turkey—once the center of Ottoman Rule. It is where the Phanariotes lived, in the Greek district of Fener. The Turkish overlords appointed them rulers of Moldavia and Wallachia. Dmitri Cantemir was selected to lead Moldavia and Constantine Brancovan to govern the neighboring southern principality of Wallachia. Since the fifteen-century, the two principalities had made large sums of payments to the Sultan in exchange for protection. Since the sum was very high, Dmitri would be forced to raise taxes in Moldavia—something he did not want to do. He was determined to follow the principles of his father Constantine Cantemir, Prince of Moldavia from 1685-1693. A good and conscientious ruler, he had protected the people from taxes and introduced peace to Moldavia.

"Before Prince Dmitri could implement his father's teachings, serious rumors reached his ears. His friend, Ambassador Peter Tolstoy of Russia, told him that Czar Peter was ready to wage a campaign against the Ottoman Turks in an effort to liberate the Balkan Christians. Dmitri made up his mind to support this effort. He had a reason for wanting to join the great Czar for he believed Ottoman power was at its end and that Moldavia would be well advised to seek protection from a more powerful ally. The Moldavian people too, were tired of being governed by the Ottomans and Dmitri knew they would support him in this decision for an independent Moldavia. Dmitri did not waste time.

"In great secrecy, in April 1711, he signed a treaty with Peter the Great to assist a Russian invasion and to provide 10,000 troops in exchange for Moldavia's independence and Russia's protection. Constantine Brancovan was aware of Prince Dmitri's plans and also agreed to join forces to assist Peter the Great against the Ottomans as they too had to pay sums of monies to the Sultan and were in a similar situation as Moldavia. As a result, men from Moldavia and Wallachia enlisted in Peter the Great's army. One regiment was made up entirely of cavalry from Moldavia and Wallachia. *The Battle of the Prut* commenced.

"The Ottoman army began its march into Moldavia, once it was known that Prince Dmitri and his principality had joined forces with the Czar. The Ottomans would not waste time. They planned to strike immediately as they considered themselves unstoppable. Cantemir was anxious and sent urgent messages to Sheremetev, the commander of the Russian army, which he wanted to move faster or to provide an advance guard of 4,000 men to protect his people from their vengeance. Peter the Great was aware of the advancement of the Ottomans and gave orders to Sheremetev to hurry and protect the principalities of Moldavia and Wallachia. The Czar, sincere in his actions and compassion, wanted to ensure the Moldavian people that the arrival of the Russians was a blessing.

"To get his message across, he had a statement printed and distributed to all the Balkan Christians, stating: *The Turks have trampled the faith of the Moldavian people, by seizing, ravaging, and destroying many churches and monasteries; they deceive; take advantage of widows and orphans. I come to your aid; do not run away from my great empire, for it is just. Do not let the Turks deceive you any longer. Do not run away from my world. Fight for faith, and fight for the church, for which we shall shed our last drop of blood.*

"The Russian troops were given strict codes of conduct for their behavior during their march across Moldavia. They were to respect the people, and anything they took they would have to pay for. Pilfering was punishable by death. The town of Iasi, the Moldavian capital on the Prut River was hit first and knowing the Russian troops would assist them, the Moldavian people flung themselves on the Turks, fighting them off. They were confident that with the great power of Russia behind them, their battle would be one of victory. They fought fearlessly, but did not have enough forces, causing many of them to be killed. Sheremetev had not yet arrived despite orders from the Czar to do so as he was behind schedule. The Moldavian army needed help desperately and Prince Dmitri begged Sheremetev not to waste time and instead to march directly to Iasi, and not to the east bank of the Prut River as originally had been planned. They wouldn't last much longer, as the Turks were strong and powerful in their endless attacks.

"Once Sheremetev arrived with his cavalry on horses, he decided not to wait for the Czar and to storm the Turks. With vigor, their forces raced across the Prut River shouting, '*Attack! Attack!*' Streams of water sprayed the horses and soldiers as they raced across the river waving their swords high above their heads. In the confusion, several horses collided and along with their riders fell into the dark waters, but surfaced immediately and carried on. The Turks surprised by this turn of events, and the aggressiveness of their enemy, retreated to the hills in order to organize and consider a new strategy. This allowed precious time for Peter the Great and his troops to reach the Prut River. The Czar, his wife Catherine I and their troops had arrived from the north west of Russia. Sheremetev and his men arrived from the north east of Russia. Finally, they were able to meet at Iasi. Once arriving, the Czar rode ahead by himself.

"A conference had been arranged with Dmitri Cantemir."

I listened to the professor's narrative of the historical battle. He is definitely touched in the head, most likely from all the history he's been studying, I surmised.

I noticed his pudgy cheeks turning red as beets when he recounted the events of the past. He had a round belly that jiggled slightly when he got excited. He wore an over-sized, wrinkled white short-sleeved shirt that overlapped onto his gray trousers that were held up by a wide brown belt. As the professor continued with his oration, I began to imagine the meeting between the two leaders, Peter the Great of Russia and Prince Dmitri Cantemir of Moldavia.

4

The Battle Conference

The Czar rode into Dmitri's camp dismounting from his horse landing with a thump on the ground. He was a man of huge stature, a natural athlete with great strength, larger than life, being just under seven feet. He took long strides and walked quickly, his arms swinging back and forth as if trying to keep pace with his feet. A birthmark on the right side of his cheek reflected prominently in the evening light.

"Welcome," said Prince Dmitri as he ran to greet the Czar. "We have been eagerly anticipating your visit. A small banquet has been prepared in your honor. Come, sit and taste some of our traditional dishes." He glanced at the Czar and then to the long table that was covered entirely with food for this monumental occasion. Dmitri knew that once the stomach was satisfied, a content person would be more agreeable in serious matters.

Peter the Great had traveled extensively and had experienced many foods, but he had never seen such spectacular dishes as the ones on this table! His eyes opened wide as he gazed on the visual display of unusual cuisine. Prince Dmitri having noticed that the Czar was in awe of such unique dishes, began to elaborate. "Let me explain our Moldavian delicacies to you. We will start with meatball soup (*perişoare*). Then, there are varieties of sausages, lamb and pig roasts, sweet bread with nuts *(rahat),* and cornmeal mush *(mamaliga)*. You must also try our Moldavian stew *(tochitura Moldoveneasca)*, and egg-plant salad *(salata de vinete)*. However, before we begin, a toast with our finest Moldavian brandy *Tuica*. It is made from the fresh plums of my fruit trees," continued Dmitri, not giving the Czar a chance to reply.

The Czar did not mind or notice. His eyes were still focused on the visual display of exotic foods.

A silver platter with two half-filled crystal glasses of *Tuica* was set on a nearby table. Dmitri handed the Czar a glass and took the other for himself. "Do as I do and you will enjoy the drink to its fullest! Now, take a deep whiff and let the aroma enter your nostrils. With that done, let's have a taste and see if that gratifies your senses," he said, as they took the drink to their mouths.

Czar Peter mimicked the prince, swirling the wine in his glass, allowing the glass to breathe in bits of oxygen. A scent of spicy forest fruits filled the air as he took the glass to his nose and inhaled. "What an unusual flavor? It is more than plums that my palate savors. What is that extraordinary taste?"

"That, dear Czar is fine tannin. It has a delicate twist of chocolate and that gives it the appeal that you are attracted to. Come let us enjoy more. Drink up! May half a glass of wine bring you a full life," he toasted the Czar, giving him a tight bear hug.

"May our *boodarcheft* drinking toast signify a harmonious and long lasting friendship," saluted Dmitri.

The Czar, although a bit perplexed, instinctively returned the jovial embrace.

Seeing that the Czar was greatly amused by the toast and festivities, Dmitri continued on with conversation. "Do we eat to live, or live to eat? It's an old Moldavian saying and with that said, let us begin to enjoy our scrumptious meal. Pofta Buna!"

Peter the Great did not pay any attention to Dmitri's words. He had already picked up a lamb shank with his tanned callused hands. He did not like formality and he had no need for it. Prince Dmitri, seeing his guest ravaging the roast, joined him, however, with fork and knife in hand. Although, Peter enjoyed the food, he grew restless and could not sit for long. He had to occasionally jump from his chair to stretch his legs. It was a habit he could not change.

There was no time to be wasted. They would begin their conference while eating. The talks were brisk, with both men easily coming to a mutual agreement. With council talks completed, Czar Peter and Dmitri signed the *Treaty of Lutsk,* stating that Moldavia would be an independent state under the protection of the Czar. Upon completion of the signing, Peter the Great stood up, shook hands with Prince Dmitri, and remarked.

"I have heard much about you Cantemir. Now, meeting with you, I can say what I have heard has been confirmed and that you are a sensible man, useful in council. I have a good impression of you."

Dmitri was pleased with ruler's compliment, which once again confirmed his abilities as an accomplished negotiator.

Peter the Great rode back to his camp. Not only was his appetite satisfied, his mind was confident of a complete victory against the Ottomans.

During this time, in Iasi, Peter received an offer of peace from the Ottomans which he rejected because he was confident he would win the battle. He had his armies around him and he had the support of Moldavia and Wallachia. This battle would surely be an easy victory for him. In this good mood Peter invited Prince Cantemir to visit his Russian army, still camped on the Prut River. There with his wife Catherine I and numerous guests, Peter the Great celebrated the second anniversary of another great victory, the battle of Poltava. Surely, he would be just as victorious in the battle against the Ottomans. As the Czar celebrated, he did not know his military situation was deteriorating. The Ottomans, informed of his rejection of the peace offer, were marching towards Iasi with an army of 200,000 men. They also had now the support of Peter's ally, ruler Constantine Brancovan of Wallachia.

Knowing the Ottomans were on the march Brancovan had switched sides to them. Just as they were ordering his arrest for treason Brancovan announced he would no longer honor any treaty signed with the Czar. He then handed over the supplies meant for the Russian army to the Ottomans. This betrayal not only would have a negative impact on the Russian Army, it would prove to be a grave error that would eventually cost Brancovan and his family their lives. Upon learning this Peter the Great still continued on. He knew the supplies lay on the lower Prut River and were not guarded so he would cross the west bank and move south. He planned to capture the Ottoman supplies and cut them off from their base.

The entire Russian army, with 12,000 horsemen, continued to the west bank and towards the rear of the Ottoman army. The infantry crossed the Prut River and began moving south down the west bank in three divisions. The first was led by General Janus, the second by the Czar, and the third by General Repin. General Janus was the first to make contact with the Ottomans. The two armies sighted each other across the river. On each side, thousands of men were lined up. The Grand Vizier leading the Ottomans became so frightened at such a sight that he considered a retreat. He had never seen enemy troops and was unsure of what to do. His advisers pressed him to continue, reassuring him, it was the only way. The Vizier accepted their recommendations and ordered the Turks to cross the river and fight.

The Czar and his division were holding a position behind a marsh. General Janus's troops, being tired, sought rest there. Without warning the Turks came up quickly from behind and began their attack. The assault continued nonstop. The Moldavian army, inexperienced as they were, strongly held their ground, but they too, were becoming tired. The Czar sent orders for Repin to bring in the third division to relieve the two that were exhausted. However, Repin's men were pinned down by Tatars, a Turkic ethnic group originally from the Mongol empire, which were aiding the Turks, and therefore were unable to do so. The Ottoman assaults continued to get stronger and Peter had no choice, but to withdraw.

As the Russians retreated, the Ottomans followed closely behind with their continual attacks. To make matters worse, the Tatars were galloping on their horses in and out among the wagons, causing many provisions to be lost; as a result the Russian army was hungry, exhausted and thirsty. They began to dig shallow trenches to protect themselves against the horsemen, who swarmed around like bees. Would this be the end of the great Czar?

The Ottomans were not finished. They began to launch a major attack. Their artillery had arrived and 300 cannons were pointed in the direction of the Russian camp. Thousands of Cossacks, military style horsemen of Eastern Slavic group and Tatars patrolled opposite sides of the riverbank for the Ottomans. With their 120,000 infantry and 80,000 cavalry, compared to the Czar's infantry of 38,000 men, the Ottomans were overwhelming.

Peter's cavalry was nowhere in sight as the Czar was pinned down, his men starving and dying of thirst. It was July and the heat was stifling. It was too dangerous to get water from the nearby river, where they were subject to intense fire from the Tatars. One of the Czar's sections was covered entirely by dead horses.

The emotional stress was taking its toll. A nervous twitch in the ruler's head erupted and his face became distorted from the pain. Not even Catherine could soothe him. She and her women were taking refuge in a shallow pit that had been dug to protect them. This could be the end. The situation seemed impossible. They looked at the thousands of Ottoman camp-fires, which seemed to go on forever, over the hills and on both sides of the river. Orange, yellow and red flames glowed against the canvass of nightfall. The Czar knew that once day broke, he would be attacked and doomed. He, who had been victorious in Poltava, would be captured by the Ottomans and most likely pulled through the streets of Istanbul in a cage. He had been too confident and too proud, and now, it had come to this. The Ottomans not only had Peter the Great, the future of Russia in their hands, they also had his wife, Catherine. What was he to do?

It should have ended in the morning, but the assaults con-tinued with open fire. The Russians prepared for the worst. The Czar was desperate. He had no choice but to order the Russians to fight and not give up. Thousands of weary Rus-sians and Moldavian cavalry got out of their trenches. They fought until they collapsed from exhaustion or were killed. Heavy losses occurred and the Russians were forced to retreat again.

It was during this retreat that some Ottoman fighters were taken prisoner. It was learned they also had encountered heavy losses and were not inclined to continue the battle. The Czar realized he had a way out. He would send an envoy to the Grand Vizer and negotiate terms of his surrender. The Czar's advisers were against this proposal, but Catherine, sensing this was the only way out persuaded him to continue.

The following terms were proposed: large bribes would be offered to the Grand Vizier, and Peter would trade away the ancient city of Azov and other Russian territories. He would agree to demolish the fortress of Taganrog, and he would recognize the King of Poland and lastly stop interfering in the affairs of the Polish-Lithuanian Commonwealth. The Vizier, hearing this proposal, decided to accept. His best men did not want to fight any longer. Furthermore, there were rumors that Hapsburg, Austria, was preparing for a war with them. The Vizer had also learned that the Russian cavalry had seized many of the Ottoman supplies and burned its gunpowder. The Vizier was ill at ease with this latest information and he decided that continuing the war was not in the best interest of any parties. He accepted the terms of Peter the Great. The Ottoman army would stand aside and let the surrounded Russian army return peacefully to Russia.

Prince Dmitri stepped out from behind the Moldavian and Russian camp to face his fellow countrymen before the act of surrender was to take place.

"My brothers, you have been taken under the wings of the Russian Czar, whom you helped in an attempt to free our tear stained ancient land. It didn't work out this time and we are unable to alleviate our country and ourselves from the clutches of the Ottomans. The great Peter has invited us to Russia. He will give us land and homes, pensions, and the right to live by our customs and our forefather's precepts. I do not force anyone. Who wishes, may remain here with their families and their homes, but those who have nowhere to go, who know that only crude Ottomans wait on the front, can come with me to Russia's boundary and its region to lead a free life. No one is forced. I say to you one more time: Make up your own minds, who wishes to stay, and who wishes to leave."

Dmitri looked among the 6,000 faces of his Moldavian brothers and continued with his statement.

"Those who wish to remain here in Moldavia, stay put. Those who wish to follow me, the Moldavian ruler, proceed to the wagons and to the Russian camp."

Two thirds of the Moldavian army stayed and another two thousand citizens decided to join the prince and the Czar in Russia, sealing their future in their choice. The treaty was signed on July 13, 1711, and the Russian army began its march out of the camp on the Prut River. Regiments of Tatar horsemen and Cossacks who had only attacked hours before, peacefully escorted them. As they marched back to their homeland, the Ottoman Vizier remarked.

"It is against Mohammad's law to deny peace to an enemy who begs it, but before I depart, I shall take Dmitri Cantemir as my captive."

The Vizer inquisitively glanced around.

"Where is he? Where is Dmitri?" he inquired. "I shall bring him back to the Sultan. Let the Sultan determine the fate of a traitor."

However, no one knew where the Prince was. He had disappeared along with his family. Dmitri's wife, Cassandra, and their six small children were hidden in Peter the Great's Imperial carriage for safety. However, Dmitri, separated during the battle, had found his way alone to the back of the wagon trains. He jumped into one of the wagons loaded with baggage belonging to Tsarina Catherine, hoping no one would look there. He hurriedly pushed the heavy wooden cases and the many sacks containing food and supplies aside. The Vizer and his men would be searching for him. He struggled to cover himself quickly with whatever he could find, as he heard footsteps approaching.

Dmitri tried not to breathe. His heart was pounding so heavy he feared it could be heard. It was hot and there was no air underneath all this baggage. He began to sweat profusely. Surely, he would suffocate in this darkness. He would die under the baggage containing the petticoats of women, instead of an honorable death on the battlefield.

It would be the ultimate insult to my country and family, he thought. Just at that moment, Dmitri heard the Czar say, "I am willing to surrender a city in hopes of winning it back later, but I shall never surrender people who have entrusted themselves to me."

"Well, let us speak of it no more. Two great empires should not prolong a war for the sake of a coward," replied the Vizier.

Unable to locate Prince Dmitri and having more important issues on his mind, the Grand Vizier departed. Catherine and her servants climbed onto the wagons. Several more Tatars on horseback appeared. They each carried a burning branch to guide the way to escort Tsarina Catherine's wagons back to the Russian Empire and unknowingly; the one Dmitri was hiding in.

The Battle of the Prut had ended. Prince Dmitri and his family had escaped. The several thousand Moldavian people who followed him, settled in Russia. Peter the Great granted favors to Prince Dmitri, giving him the title of Russian prince and granting him large estates.

Cantemir's Moldavia was not so lucky. The Tatars ravaged the towns and villages, setting them on fire.

The Vizier had won the battle of the Prut. Peter the Great lost territories. Dmitri Cantemir lost his homeland. Constantine Brancovan was to lose the most. The ruler of Wallachia had first betrayed the Sultan, then the Czar. The Ottomans could never trust him again. He knew that and was prepared to flee. He had sent large amounts of money to banks in Western Europe. His confidence overshadowed his good judgment and in time caused his plans to be tragically interrupted, for he would be caught and imprisoned by the Ottomans.

5

Hints of Royalty

My daydream of the battle abruptly ended when I almost fell out of my seat.

"This is boring, and I am tired of looking at that map. My personal viewpoint of the battle is much more exciting than the professor's," I grumbled on to no one in particular.

"Our name is very famous in Russian history!"

"What, papa? What did you say? I don't understand."

"I said our name is very famous in Russia," papa repeated patiently.

He always managed to say the unexpected at the most unforeseen moment.

"Our name is well known? What do you mean, papa?" I asked.

"The surname we are using is not our true name. In Germany, I took another name in order to protect my identity and avoid retribution from the communists. Karanowytsch is not our real name."

"Then, what is our last name?" I asked pressing the issue further.

"I cannot tell you, but our name is just as well known in Russia as is George Washington in America," replied father. "If one mentions our name in Russia, everyone will know of it."

I did not know what to make of papa's statement. Was it a story, a fable, or was it for real? I tried hard to think of the many notable Russian names I knew, wondering which belonged to my family. Why would her father not tell her? What was the big secret? They were in America now. His actions in Germany were a long time ago. Why should he be still so concerned? What was Boris Karanowytsch hiding? What would our true surname name reveal? Was there a past connection with the name that would explain his present peculiar behavior? I shrugged my shoulders, disappointed not knowing what to think. Little did I realize there was a reason for papa's remark, and that the answer to my question was staring me directly in the face. A curious person, I turned my head to glance back at the map. Was there any connection? No! Surely, not Peter the Great!

"Kantemir," papa whispered into my ear, as he made his way past me and out of sight.

Puzzled and perplexed, I got up from my seat not paying much attention to what papa had just said. I was just happy that the history lesson was finally over. I skipped over to the lunch area, but it was early and food was not available. I noticed the group of older men from the history class huddled around a tall handsome man. The man was dressed in a navy blue suit and wore a tie; a light blue handkerchief was neatly folded in his suit pocket. He wore a ring on his small finger and he looked so distinguished. He was answering the many questions asked of him. I observed he was polite and well-mannered despite the barrage of inquiries. Papa was there too, squeezed in among the older men. He had managed to be everywhere and into everything and yet at times nowhere to be found. I had to approach him and ask more questions.

"Papa, who is he?" I asked tugging away at his sleeve.

"That is Prince Golitsyn," he replied. I looked at papa. He was in a trance and obviously in awe of the prince, but his look of admiration was so different from the rest of the men that without much thought and to my own surprise I asked.

"Papa, are we related to Prince Golitsyn?"

Without taking his eyes off the prince, papa's only reply was, "A long time ago, ours married theirs."

I wondered how papa knew all of this, but I didn't question it. What I did not realize was that he had revealed another clue to our ancestral name and that name would implicate him in being more than just a volunteer in joining a fight against the communists during World War II.

Forty years would pass before I was able to solve the mystery of papa's involvement with the Russian Liberation Movement.

6

Camp Ballet

The summer days of 1963 quickly flew by. The camp's activities kept everyone busy. Volleyball, ping-pong, games of chess, and swimming occupied most of the camper's time. I had managed to squeeze in ballet lessons. Special arrangements were made for me to take dance classes from a former ballerina with the *Ballet Russe de Monte Carlo*. Today I would along with my fellow camper, Zina, take the short walk alongside the dirt road that would lead us to the two story home of Madame for our weekly dance class.

"Come on, Zina. Try to catch me," I shouted as I ran to the woods alongside the roadway.

"You, better come out of there. There is a lot of poison ivy about. I'm not going in there after you," replied Zina.

We walked arm in arm until we reached a narrow cobbled path, lined with trees that led to the home. Even though, the house was old and in need of repair, there was a magical quality associated with it. The house enveloped character, personality, charm, and I sensed a story to go along with it.

There in the arched doorway, stood Madame. She was waving her hand. "Dobryy-dyen, come in girls, come in. We can get started immediately. I have been anxiously waiting for you ballerinas." An elderly man who introduced himself as Madame's husband when we entered further greeted us.

"Welcome, fellow dancers. I was once a performer myself. Now, you see me, cane in my hand and an old man, but when I was young I was an important figure in the *Ballet Russe*. Here, look. I want to show you girls as I was," he said proudly.

Zina and I looked at a photograph of a handsome ballet dancer supporting a ballerina in an execution of an *arabesque*.

"This is how we met. We were both dancers with the company," he continued.

"My husband does not have many visitors. The first chance he has, he will bore you with his stories. Please excuse him," interrupted Madame.

"Mischka, enough of that, the girls have come here to take ballet class and not listen to your stories of long ago," said Madame.

I did not mind, nor did Zina. We wanted to hear, firsthand, the story of the *Ballet Russe de Monte Carlo* from an original cast member. It was not often one gets such a chance. We had great admiration for these two extraordinary elderly dancers. I understood now why the house had so much character. The quintessence of their characters transposed to the home.

"We have much work to do. Let's get started with *pliés* at the barre. Come this way. My small studio is in the basement," said Madame.

Zina and I followed Madame, a petite delicate lady, her hair pulled back in a bun with large spectacles resting on her nose. Although, well into her sixties, she still had the persona of a ballerina. We made our way down the stairs, our eyes barely adjusted to the darkness of the stairwell, when a bright light came on.

"There, that's much better," said Madame, taking her hand off the wall switch.

I looked around the room. One wall was entirely covered up with a huge mirror. Another wall on the opposite side of the room had a ballet barre attached to it. An old brown piano stood to the side on the wooden floor. Madame walked over to the piano and picked up a pair of tattered point shoes that lay on top.

"These were the last shoes I danced in," she said. "These other shoes over there are the ones worn by Anna Pavlova. Look, her signature is on them."

Putting the shoes aside, she picked up another photograph.

"These are my fellow members of the *Ballet Russe*; I'm on the right side."

I looked at the photograph. Madame certainly hadn't changed much.

The sound of music filled the room. Madame had turned on the record player.

"*Pliés*, pozhaluysta, and a one and a two." Her voice hovered over the music, her cane hitting the floor in tune with the notes.

I returned the photograph and took my place at the barre.

Dance classes continued the entire summer. We eagerly looked forward to Madame's classes along with the stories of her ballet years. Madame had a strict, but soft, touch when it came to teaching. She was feared, yet admired, a trait often shared by distinguished dance teachers.

The last days at camp were fast approaching. I was playing ping-pong when I noticed Madame enter the camp. Immediately, I dropped my paddle and ran off to greet her. It was not often that Madame came to the camp.

"Hello, Madame. How nice to see you," I said.

"Nice to see you as well, my dear. I have great news," replied Madame.

"This Saturday we have an invitation for tea. We are going to my friend's home. Alexandra Danilova has invited us to be her guests. We have remained friends all this years, since we first danced together with the *Ballet Russe*. Make sure you and Zina are ready and on time. We cannot keep Ms. Danilova waiting. I will pick you up at 2:00p.m."

Saturday arrived and at exactly 2:00p.m. an old rattled car arrived at camp. Behind the wheel of the dilapidated green Buick sat Madame looking very serious.

"Come on, girls, get in," she said.

Zina and I jumped in the back of the car giggling at each other as we made our way in. We couldn't imagine Madame driving a car. She was barely visible, peering over the steering wheel through her thick spectacles. We could tell she was not an experienced driver as the car made its way along the narrow road of the township of Jackson. We gripped each other's hand tightly as Madame made an abrupt right turn and into a driveway of another older house, even more charming than Madame's home.

"We are here! Girls, I must remind you. Do not speak, unless you are spoken to. Know your manners and know your place!" she exclaimed.

"Is she so renowned? Must we not say a word?" I whispered.

"Alexandra Danilova is a great dancer and legend. We need to be respectful," answered Zina, who was well familiar with all aspects of the dance world—professional and private. I dared say no more. We followed Madame to the rear of the two storied home and through a beautiful garden filled with roses. Straight ahead, at a table sat a gracious petite lady. Although, tiny in stature, she radiated a grand presence. A white porcelain teapot etched with pink roses sat on a white-laced tablecloth in the center of the table.

"Come, be seated," commanded Ms. Danilova.

Zina and I obediently sat down. Intuitively, we smoothed out the crinkles in our dresses. We remembered Madame's instructions and remained silent. Madame and Ms. Danilova exchanged kisses, followed by greetings of "Zdrahstvooytee, Zdrahstvooytee." Madame sat down between Zina and me. The housekeeper, Miss Twysden poured tea into the matching teacups that were set in front of us. I noticed she wore a white ruffled apron with pink roses, which matched the tea set. I found this quite amusing. I grinned at Zina, who did not take notice for she was still nervously smoothing her dress.

"Sugar, milk?" inquired Madame.

Everyone took milk in their tea, as was the Russian custom. Zina and I remained quiet. We just listened as the two former dancers chatted and relived their dancing past.

"George Balanchine and I have remained dear friends all these years. As a matter of fact, it is because of George I have my present position at the School of American Ballet," said Ms. Danilova fondly. She glanced at Zina and me.

"Madame has spoken of your dedication and hard work in your ballet studies. I am offering you two girls a scholarship to take classes at the American School of Ballet in New York City," she said.

Honored at the attention bestowed upon me, I sat up straight. I didn't want to miss a word. I have not felt this special since my childhood days in Germany. I could see Madame was beaming as the words were spoken. Did she know of this in advance? We could not believe our ears at what we just heard and what was offered to us. We gazed at each other and squeezed hands underneath the table. We only dared to say,

"Spasibo, Ms. Danilova." Our words were acknowledged with a grin from both ladies.

"We must go now. It's time to return to camp. I promised I would have you girls back before dinner," said Madame. Everyone stood up and began to make their way to the car.

"Dosvidaniya, Ms. Danilova and thank you again," I said.

"Work hard, girls, work hard," was the reply.

I had to take one more look at the great ballerina as we were leaving. I glanced back to see Ms. Danilova standing next to her roses. It was late afternoon and the sun radiated behind her tiny figure. She appeared as if performing on stage. She raised her hand to wave farewell. Yes, she still commanded the spotlight, even off stage.

"Do you realize what a great honor you have been granted? Not only tea with the great Danilova, but a scholarship, too!" said Madame as she opened the car door.

"Yes," replied Zina. "We shall never forget this day!"

Summer passed as fast as it had arrived. Most of the campers had left. The camp was practically deserted. It was a sad occasion for me for I had made many friends. Now, I would have to part with them for another year. Most of all, I would miss Madame, who had come to Camp P.O.R.R. especially to say her good-byes.

"Dosvidaniya, my dearest friends Olga and Zina," I said as I hugged my two best friends. I walked over to Madame and gave her three kisses as was the custom. "Spasibo, Madame. I will never forget all that you have done."

Slowly, one by one, the campers and their families departed. The dirt road leaving Camp P.O.R.R. would take them onto the main highway and to new crossroads of life.

While circumstances didn't permit me to move to New York City, the offer of a scholarship boosted my self-confidence and gave me permission to delve into my father's intrigue.

7

Nicholas: End of Summer, 1963

E ven though I enjoyed camp, I was happy to be home again.
I missed my American life. I immediately ran to my room.
"Hello, Connie Stevens! Hello Troy Donahue!" I said, looking at their pictures on the wall above my bed before reaching into my dresser drawer to retrieve my transistor radio. I
returned to my world just as I had left it and back to the arms
of rock and roll. I spent the next few hours listening to the
new top hits I had missed while away at camp: *The End of the
World* by Skeeter Davis; *Rhythm of the Rain* by the Cascades;
Hey Paula by Paul and Paula; *Blue Velvet* by Bobby Vinton; and,
He's So Fine by the Chiffons. I could have listened all night, had
mother not interrupted me.

"Go to bed early Ella. Tomorrow we are going to Patterson,
New Jersey to visit your father's friend and his family. We
shall be spending a night there."

The announcement of an unexpected trip caught me by
surprise. School was about to begin in a few days, but I was

ready for more adventure. At least I could take my transistor along with me this time. I hummed along with my favorite song, *My Boyfriends Back and There's Gonna be Trouble*, a song by the Angels—that I knew by heart. I lay in bed with my radio pressed against my ear as was my nightly custom. I fell asleep listening to the sounds of the Beach Boys' *Surfer Girl*.

The next morning our entire family boarded the Greyhound bus from Jimmy's Smoke Shop on West Main Street, the transport hub in New Britain. I took a seat by the window. As the bus departed I pretended that I was returning to camp to start the summer all over again. The lulling noise of the bus made me drowsy and before I knew it I had dozed off. It was not too long before I heard mother say, "Wake-up, we are here."

We had arrived at Nicholas's home. Nicholas and papa were friends from Germany and had arrived in America at about the same time. That was all I knew and that was all papa was willing to tell me. Nicholas and his wife, Nina had a lovely home. A huge backyard with a picnic table caught my eye, as I stretched my neck to take a look at the side of the house.

"We will be dining outside in the fresh air, summer is not over yet!" exclaimed Nicholas with a twinkle in his eye as he looked at me and the other children. "Hooray, hooray," everyone yelled, jumping up and down with joy.

I dropped my small bag of clothing and immediately ran to the backyard. A long picnic table was covered with a blue and white-checkered tablecloth. A mix of colorful flowers, freshly picked from the yard, were put in blue vases and placed on the table. Nina took chairs from inside the house and placed them alongside. Platefuls of ethnic food followed; assorted dumplings (*pirogi*), cucumbers, tomatoes, hamburgers *(katlety)*, and barbecued lamb on skewers *(shaslik)* were placed on the table.

Lively music coming from the house caught my attention and it even stopped the chatter of the playful children for a moment. The music was getting closer and it was coming from Nicholas. He was playing an accordion, his right hand striking the keys and the other rapidly pushing small buttons on the opposite side of the instrument. An energetic mood set in prompting all to gather together, lock arms and form a large circle. Everyone began to sing a traditional Russian song, *Kalinka, Kalinka, Kkalinka, Moya* in tune with the music. I could not contain myself any longer. I jumped in the center of the circle and with a twirl of a spin began to perform a Russian folk dance. As the tempo increased, I danced faster and faster to keep pace. The faster I danced, the faster everyone clapped. A series of pirouette turns ended simultaneously with the music and concluded the dance. I dropped down on the grass to catch my breath. I lay there, breathing heavily and looking up at the many stars above.

"Bravo, bravo, well done! Excellent job, you must all be hungry. Get up Ella. Let's all go and eat," Nicholas stated as he laughed.

Everyone scrambled to the table. Eating and conversation carried on well into the late night hours. It seemed odd that during the entire evening not a word was mentioned of the long-standing friendship between Nicholas and papa, even though, supposedly they were close friends. They seemed to avoid bringing up any reminisces of their past lives as friends.

Maybe, things are best forgotten and left alone, but for the moment all shall find pleasure and contentment in the last days of summer, I thought.

8

An Autumn Murder

"They found him, they found him!" Papa was nervously pacing about the room, panting, and almost out of breath.

"What, papa, what happened?" I ran from my room feeling nervous from the tone of papa's voice.

"They found him and they killed him. They killed Nicholas. I knew it! It would only be a matter of time! I shall be next!" he ranted on.

"Who?" I asked. I was terrified for I had never seen papa so alarmed.

"They said it was an accident! No! It was not an accident! The Soviet Secret Police found him and killed him," he continued on adamantly.

I could not believe what I had just heard! Kind Nicholas, who was so full of life and who only a few months ago entertained our family, was dead. Why would anyone kill him and why were foreign operatives involved? Had papa been overly affected by the devastating news? Would papa be next as he stated? This was America. How could it be possible? I saw that papa was shaken up, but I had to ask more questions. I had to learn more of the circumstances of Nicholas's death.

"What happened, papa? How could what you are saying happen, here in this country?" I asked.

"You don't know anything, *Ellatchka*," said papa addressing me by my affectionate name.

"They are unstoppable. They do dreadful deeds, evil deeds, anywhere, even in this country. They said it was a terrible accident, but I know better. They said Nicholas was crushed to death by a crane he was operating. He was an expert crane operator. It just isn't possible. I don't believe it. No one believes it, not even Nina, his wife. It was a carefully executed murder!"

I listened intently to papa's account of Nicholas's demise. He rarely gave details of our family background or circumstances of his life before I was born. I did not doubt papa's word that Nicholas's death was a premeditated murder and I was scared. I was scared for papa and I was scared for my family.

"Nina told me what occurred, the night Nicholas was killed," papa began. Everyone listened intently.

"It was a Friday night. Nicholas had ended his shift at the construction site and returned home. He had just finished eating dinner with his family when the telephone rang."

"Hello? What! An emergency at this hour! It cannot wait until tomorrow morning? It's too dark for any repairs! What! You say I am the only one who can solve the problem? Very well; I'm not keen on going out at this hour, but if I must, I must," replied Nicholas, pressing his cheek against the telephone.

"Nicholas, what is the problem?" asked Nina, as Nicholas returned the telephone to the receiver.

"I am needed at the construction site. There seems to be a malfunction with the crane. I am needed immediately. I need to go or the entire project will be postponed and put the company behind schedule. It will be over a million dollar loss if I don't help."

"No, Nicholas, don't go tonight. I beg you! It is not a good idea," pleaded Nina.

"No, I must! I have promised."

"At least tell me who called," said Nina.

"I did not get his name, but he appeared to be one of the senior production staff. I cannot say no."

"I don't feel comfortable with what you are telling me," said Nina. "Please, don't go."

"No, Nina I must," replied Nicholas.

"Very well, I can see it will do no good arguing with you. I will get your warm brown jacket. It looks like it's going to be an early snowfall this year. The sky is all gray and it's beginning to cloud up. Don't forget your gloves, too."

"Don't worry, Nina. I'll be home soon. Then we can enjoy a nice cup of hot tea." With that said, Nicholas picked up the metal box, containing his tools, and went out the door.

The construction site was deserted when Nicholas arrived. The site overlooked the murky waters of the Hudson River. New York City was just across the river and Nicholas could see the glow of the city lights. But here, at the site, it was dark and cold. He could not see anything or anyone.

"Hello, anyone there?" he shouted out. There was no reply.

"I must have arrived a bit too early. No one is here yet," Nicholas muttered aloud.

"Never the less, I shall get started."

He took a flashlight from his toolbox. He could see the outline of the crane. It was huge and in the dark of the night it looked like a monster. He cautiously approached the crane for a closer look. Nothing was visible. He would have to shine his flashlight towards the right corner of the compartment to check for any loose wiring.

"Ah!"

And then there was silence. Nicholas had no time to scream, no time to respond. It happened so fast. He did not feel any pain. He fell to the ground as the crane toppled on him. All that was evident of a human being was a flashlight thrown not far from the crane, its light still on, shining towards the direction of the city lights of Manhattan.

The winter morning sun shinned on the fresh snow. It had snowed the entire night, burying parts of the city. Two young boys, ages twelve and fourteen were excited about the first snowfall of the season. Being a Saturday, there was no school. They were going to have fun and find adventure.

"Let's go to the construction site around the corner. No one will be there today," said Jimmy, the older boy.

Jimmy and Tommy put on their down jackets, gloves, hats and boots. They were in a hurry, anxious to enjoy the snow and eagerly dashed outdoors. They were ready for anything! They ran fast and were out of breath when they reached the site. Their cheeks turned rosy red and even though they wore wool hats, their ears were red from the cold wind.

"Look, what I found, a flashlight! It's still on," said Tommy.

Jimmy was not paying attention. His eyes were focused on the huge yellow crane partly covered in snow, lying on its side. Something seemed amiss. Jimmy continued to stare. He could not see anything. He crept forward for a closer look. An arm in a brown jacket was protruding from underneath the crane.

"Run, Tommy. Let's get out of here!"

"A bad accident, that's all, very unfortunate," said the authorities as they departed Nina's home after informing her of the accident.

Nina stood in the doorway, tears rolling down her face.

"I told him not to go, I told him. Why did he have to be so stubborn? No, it was not an accident. The call came from his company, but no one had any knowledge of such a call being placed. All our equipment is in working order, no problems with any cranes. Even the one in the accident was in perfect working order, they said."

No one had an explanation for the curious demise of Nicholas. That is, no one except his old friend, Boris, my father. After Nina called him to tell him of Nicholas's tragic death, the only explanation he gave was, "the past has finally caught up with Nicholas." But, what past? What was done to merit such a death? The one person who knew the truth dare not say more, except, "I shall be next."

After that fateful day, I noticed papa looking over his shoulder. He said he was afraid the Soviet Secret Police or the KGB would find him and kill him, too. Or worse yet, he might be extradited to the Soviet Union and hanged as had been a few of his friends. He was cautious when answering the telephone and did not speak to anyone he did not know. He would only say, "If I die in an accident, it is not an accident." It all sounded melodramatic to me, but knowing papa I did not doubt his words.

"Papa, why do you say such things?" I asked.

"What I say is true. I cannot tell you more," he answered.

That night, in bed, I overheard papa and mother whispering.

"Nicholas was another casualty and he certainly will not be the last one. They will track down all the members of the Russian Liberation Army. They will have us all killed or sent back to the Soviet Union and hanged like General Vlasov, the leader. We are labeled as traitors and the KGB will not rest until they find us."

"Boris, there are too many members of the Russian Liberation Army for them to track down. What's done is done. They are not interested in catching all," I heard mother reply.

"The KGB and the communist government of the Soviet Union is very much interested in me, Dina, I assure you. I was instrumental. That is all you need to know," answered papa.

Boris Ivanovich's suspicions proved to be true. Unknown to him, the KGB was already hot on his trail.

9

A Soviet Tour — Summer, 1967

I was looking forward to a tour of the Soviet Union. The tour made me nervous, but it was a trip I was looking forward to as were my parents. I had no idea of what to expect. I had heard all kinds of stories and they were not good. Visitors were known not to return. I was worried that might happen to me. Still, I carried on and arrived extra early at the international terminal at John F. Kennedy Airport in New York. To my surprise, my parents were waiting at the airline counter. They had traveled from Connecticut just to send me off. This was an important event, not just for me, but for my parents as well.

"Papa, mama, you came all the way from Connecticut to see me off! It was not necessary for you to come all that distance just for a short time," I said to them.

Mother smiled and papa gave me a hug.

"This is a major trip, Ella. You are going back to our country. A country I long to return to, but it is impossible. You are the first family member to go to my birthplace to visit my homeland and the country of our ancestors," papa said.

As usual an urge overcame me to ask questions of papa's past in Russia, but what would I ask? I had no idea where to begin. If I did question him, I knew he would not elaborate, he never did. When he did disclose bits and pieces of his protective past, only more questions arose that went unanswered. I would have to wait for papa as I always did, to divulge more when he was ready.

"I want to give you some advice when you arrive in the Soviet Union. If anyone asks if you are Russian, say no. If you say you are Russian, they have every right to keep you there. You do not hold citizenship of any country. Do not take the chance," he said.

"Papa, don't frighten me. No one will pay any attention to me. Why should the Soviets want to keep a young girl? Don't be silly, papa. I have no secrets, unlike you," I answered giving him an affectionate smile accompanied by a big hug. It was then that my eyes shifted to the tattoo on his left hand. I had seen it many times before. It never interested me and as a result, I never thought to question it. It was just a tattoo. Today, for some reason, it caught my curiosity, this tattoo of a wavy dark-haired man in ancient dress. I felt it was important as it was out of character for the present century. Papa had only his left arm, the right one was lost during World War II, when he was forced to work on the roads in Austria and in Germany where shrapnel had hit his right arm. Gangrene set it and his arm had to be amputated. Strange, it was not the left hand that was hit. Was there a meaning in the tattoo on his remaining arm waiting to be discovered?

"Papa, who is that tattoo of on your hand?" I couldn't help but ask.

I could see the astonishment in his face, taken aback by

my unanticipated question. All he could do was muster, "It is someone from a very long time ago," with a wide grin on his face and a twinkle in his eye.

Well, that is something I could see for myself, I thought.

That was papa's usual reply and one that prompted for another question; however, I did not have time to be more persistent. A terminal announcement indicated my flight was ready to board.

"This is a boarding announcement for Pan American Airways flight 209 to Moscow. The flight is now ready for boarding at gate 103. All passengers are requested to proceed to the gate for immediate boarding."

"Dosvidaniya, dosvidaniya," I shouted as I ran through the terminal waving goodbye.

It was a few hours into the flight. I looked out the airplane window. There was nothing to be seen except for a few scattered white clouds that filled the skies. I fell asleep for what seemed only a couple of hours when an announcement woke me.

"Our flight has now entered Soviet airspace," was the stern in-flight broadcast from the captain.

Was that a greeting or a warning? What a nice way to be welcomed to the Soviet Union! I thought. Nothing looked or felt unusual, but that was the problem. The Soviets didn't like anyone in their airspace. More thoughts filled my head. Maybe the aircraft is going to be shot down.

What if the airline didn't submit the proper permit to fly over the U.S.S.R? It was the heated 60's and anything was possible with the cold war between the United States and the Soviet Union. I held my breath, waiting and wondering if the plane would land safely. I looked around the cabin and saw very few passengers. It was calm. No one seemed too concerned. Much to my surprise, the aircraft touched down without incident. I breathed a sigh of relief when the plane made its way down the tarmac and taxied on to the main terminal at Sheremetyevo International Airport in Moscow.

Little did I know that my relief would not last. I proceeded to the immigration hall of the small airport. I walked toward an immigration officer at a booth and took my documents out of my purse for inspection. There was a small mirror behind me, high on the wall. I did not like it. I felt the mirror was spying on me and it intimidated me. The mirror captured my every move. I felt like a criminal. My breathing became shallow and I felt myself gasping for air. I tried to be calm as I handed my re-entry permit along with my Soviet visa to the official. As I did, I noticed numerous uniformed officials standing about solemnly in the hall, expressionless, emotionless, appearing as if statues. They were doing nothing but standing and watching.

How depressed they all look. I shall not allow them to affect my mood, I thought as the officer was inspecting my documents. He opened his mouth as if to yawn and then a big wide smile appeared on his face. A gold tooth was visible next to a big dark gap where there should have been another tooth. Something is amiss. Why is he smiling? Maybe, I am in trouble and he is happy about it. He seemed to be amused. The officer looked up at me and then down at the document on his desk. He addressed me in Russian.

"Eleonora Borisovna, are you Russian?"

Oh, no, I thought remembering papa's words of advice. How could he possibly know I would be asked such a question, the first question after my arrival in the Soviet Union? He knows his fellow countrymen well!

"No, I was born in Germany," I was quick to reply.

"Is your father Russian?" he continued.

"Yes," I answered.

"Is your mother Russian?" he asked continuing with his inquiry.

"Yes," I replied again. The officer laughed out loud. "Then you are Russian! Your father is Russian. Your mother is Russian. You have Russian bloodline in your veins. You are a sly one with your answers. Go ahead, you may go," he said. He continued to shake his head and laugh.

I didn't say a word. I was fearful of being kept in the Soviet Union and never seeing my family again if I didn't quickly leave. The immigration officer might change his mind. After all, I was stateless. Although, I did hold a U.S. permanent green card, a re-entry permit with a visa was my only official document. As a refugee arriving in the United States as a child, I was a citizen of nothing. I didn't have a country and the Soviets were known to keep nationals of Russian origin, never to be heard from again, only to disappear into oblivion. I was anyone's game.

I quickly dashed off with my suitcase in hand, my legs ahead of my body, scurrying down the hall as fast as I could. I couldn't run fast enough to exit the doors of immigration. The double-glassed doors stared at me. I stared back to see my reflection. I pushed the doors open and at that moment, an entire new world exposed itself, a world so foreign, yet so familiar. An overwhelming feeling of familiarity overcame me and I felt at home in a country that I had never stepped foot in. My first thought was to find my sister that I was told about so long ago, but where would I begin? I did not have any idea where to start. Were there telephone books in Russia? I did not even know the city where my sister lived. I could start with the only address that I had—the one in Cherkessk, Russia. There were indications my sister had moved to another city, Baku. If that proved to be true, it would be difficult for me as I was in Moscow, a long distance away from Baku. It would not be easy to find her. Better to start the search tomorrow, after a day's rest.

The morning air was fresh. I finished my breakfast of a hard-boiled egg, black bread and coffee. I walked out the front entrance of the Rossiya Hotel and decided to take a stroll to the park across the street. It would give me a chance to explore and enjoy Moscow's peculiar atmosphere. I needed to clear my thoughts and this would give me the opportunity to do so. It was only a matter of seconds that I heard footsteps behind me. It was my second day in the city. Was it possible that I was already being followed? I stopped and turned around to see a man of medium build, dressed in a beige trench coat. The fedora hat on his head was pulled down, slightly concealing his eyes. He pretended not to notice me, passing by briskly. My keen sense, a trait probably inherited from papa made me feel that this strange person was suspicious. He could follow me all he wanted. It did not matter, for I didn't know where I was going or what I was going to do. It was a mystery to me too. All I knew was that I had to get away. I decided to hail a taxi. Let him keep up with that!

"Driver, are there telephone books? I am trying to locate a relative," I asked as I got into the taxi.

The driver appeared to be surprised by my inquiry. He noticed instantly I was a foreigner by my question and appearance. He had nothing to do, business was slow; I knew he would accommodate me. He would be expecting a large tip and some chewing gum. I heard there was no chewing gum in the Soviet Union and the citizens depended on the foreigners for that. I came well prepared.

"I will drive you to the police station," said the taxi driver.

"What! Why would we be going there?" His remark made me very uneasy and I wondered if I had made the correct decision to hail down this taxi to get away from being followed. I might have gotten myself into a worse predicament.

"Do you want to find your relative? The police station has

records on file of who lives where, current records," the driver continued.

I was taken aback, yet I was determined to find my sister. We drove to a police station. I handed the driver a paper with my sister's name and last known address. I waited outside, in the taxi as the driver entered the police station. It was only a matter of minutes when he came out and said sympathetically.

"Your relative does not reside at the address you gave me. The police will not release any other information, except to say she lives in another region."

I did not know what to do. I was stumped. All I could say was "Please drive me back to my hotel."

I handed the driver the two neckties that papa gave me to distribute as gifts, along with a small bottle of vodka and paid my fare.

"Spasibo, spasibo!" exclaimed the driver, happy that he had made the correct decision to invest in a profitable time. He did not get his chewing gum, but vodka was better.

I did not know that my sister, who was living in Baku, was preparing to attend a ballet program at about the same time. She had heard an American dance company from New York was in Baku. She would take this opportunity to pass a gift and message to her American sister. She was nervous as she put a small bottle of perfume with a note attached to it in her handbag. She would pass it to one of the members of the dance company after the show. She did not speak English, but with the address on note they should surmise it needed to be forwarded. She took her six-year-old son Mischa by the hand and headed to the theater. The music was lively and dramatic, but she could not concentrate on the long ballet.

The American Ballet Theater had staged *Don Quixote* in four acts that seemed to go on forever. She was anxiously waiting for it to end, as she had devised a strategy. It would not be easy to approach a member of the dance company. She would look for the dancer with the most compassionate face to help accomplish her mission. When the performance ended, she ran to the side door of the theater where the dancers would be exiting. She stood there as they passed her by, scrutinizing their faces for the right one. Maybe this one, no that one! She would have to act fast and slip the package with its note before anyone noticed. She anxiously waited for the right moment. When she saw a petite dark haired ballerina that might comply, she immediately reached out to her.

It was at that moment that a large, strong, burly arm darted out to stop her. The arm belonged to a muscular man with a deep scowl on his face. Her heart skipped a beat and she thought she would faint. She would be dragged off, along with her son and never be seen or heard from, just like her grandmother, Maria, who was exiled to Siberia. She quickly grabbed her son by the hand and ran as fast as she could to get away. It was more dangerous than she had anticipated.

Her American sister would not be getting her gift.

10

Vse, Chto Bylo eto Vse, Chto Proshlo

I was excited, for today would include an excursion to an architectural estate outside of Moscow. Tsaritsyno once known as Chornaya Graz or Black Dirt belonged to Catherine the Great. She renamed the estate *Tsaritsyno*, after purchasing it in 1777. She then had a new palace built for her by architect Vasili Bazhenov, only to have it partly torn down in 1786. Many of the estate's architectural ensembles still stood, and now the grounds were a park open to the public.

"The original building was of neo-Gothic style built in the sixteen century," said the Soviet guide as she began her presentation. "The sixteen century saw Tsarina Irina, sister of Czar Boris Gudunov, as owner. It was given to the Moldavian Prince Dmitri Kantemir in 1712 as a gift. Kantemir and his family sought refuge here after the loss of the *Battle of the*

Prut. The Prince brought along several thousand Moldavian countrymen. Greenhouses were built and exotic fruits were grown. A grand estate developed and it became a paradise on the banks of the Gorodnya River. It was home to the Kantemir family for over 60 years before Sergei Kantemir sold it to Catherine the Great in 1777."

My mind began to swirl. I recalled my history class on Peter the Great and the *Battle of the Prut* when I attended the Russian camp during the summers. I was standing on the actual historical grounds that I once studied about. I could not help but imagine how the estate must have been in 1712.

"My dear friend, your Sereneness Prince Dmitri Kantemir. Your people and country have suffered and lost much. Words can never express or show my gratitude. I can only offer you a new beginning, in a new country. I am granting you the title of "Knaz" (Prince) of the Russian Empire. You are a wise, just man. I respect your learned ways. I need an adviser. You will be my new Chancellor. Furthermore, by personal decree, I give you the estate of Black Dirt (Chornaya Graz) in compensation for the lands lost in Moldavia. You and your fellow citizens can live there peacefully. It cannot take the place of what was, but will give you a calm life in a new land. The estate of Black Dirt, with all of its villages, lands and forests all belong to you. You and your countrymen will live there in peace and comfort," the Czar proclaimed.

Black Dirt, with its rough terrain, plentiful rivers and streams with surrounding ponds became a haven for the Kantemirs, (who now used the Russian spelling of Kantemir) and the several Moldavian citizens who followed them into exile. They built greenhouses and grew fruits of their homeland. Lemons, wild oranges, peaches, pears, figs and grapes were cultivated. Soon, a splendid estate arose on the steep banks of the Gorodnya River. Festive flower gardens flourished. A square island was built on one of the ponds, with a stair leading to it along the bank. The island was situated in one of the many parks on the grounds.

Nearby, on a round hill, its ledges covered with trees and overlooking the pond was a pergola. It was called, Kantemirovka. Close by on the estate stood a stone church, dedicated to the Icon of *Our Lady of Life-Giving Spring*. Its shapes and architectural designs were Baroque in style. It had a dining hall and a two level bell tower and on one side of the church was a chapel of St. Demetrius.

Prince Dmitri Kantemir, his wife Cassandra, and their six young children, Princess Maria age twelve, Princess Smaragda (Emerald) eleven, the Princesses, Constantine nine, Matvei eight, Sergei five and Antioch four, began their new life at the estate. The minutest care was bestowed on the children. They had the best tutors assigned to instruct them in their education. The children became fluent in Greek, Turkish, Moldavian, French, Italian, Latin, and English. Ivan Ilinsky taught them the Russian language. Little Antioch was personally tutored by the Greek priest, Anastasi Kondoidi, and was introduced to classical literature at an early age. Kondoidi was instrumental in Antioch's first attempts at poetry at even such a young age.

Princess Maria was given voice and music lessons. She became an accomplished harpsichordist and was well known in Russia for her vocal talents, often singing, Italian-flavored European classics, favored by the upper classes. She performed in Europe as a singer virtuoso and harpsichordist. She toured often and became celebrated for her musical talents. On festive occasions, Prince Dmitri and Princess Maria often performed together at Chornaya Graz. Their music ranged from Moldavian dance tunes to the Ottoman and European classics;

father and daughter performing together, tanbur and harpsichord in harmony, uniting the musicality of the east and west with exotic blended tunes.

This spring Maria was home after a European tour and looking forward to spending time with her family. Plans had been made to visit the Repins. The Kantemir family had not seen them since the battle at the Prut River in Moldavia.

"Please ask the coachman to bring the carriage to the front entrance of the house. We are ready to depart. The Repins are expecting us shortly," said Cassandra.

"Mama, the carriage is already waiting for us. We are all waiting for you," replied Maria. Being the eldest, she took her mother by the arm and escorted her to the carriage. The carriage doors were wide open allowing the Kantemir children to climb to the rear seats with little Antioch leading the way. Maria, her mother and Smaragda followed the children. Maria assisted her mother to the front seat next to Smaragda. The sisters were one year apart and the oldest of the children. Their mother depended upon them as if they were responsible for the entire household. With everyone in, the carriage followed the long dirt road of the estate and out into the desolate countryside.

"Welcome, welcome!" It's a pleasure to see you and your family, Princess Cassandra. My, how the children have grown since I last saw them at the battle. How are they adjusting to their new life in our country?" asked General Repin as he led the way to the drawing room.

"They are all fine, thank you General. The children are busy with their education and learning the Russian language," replied Cassandra.

"Fine, fine, splendid! We have taken the liberty to also invite Princess Pascovia Narischkyn to our gathering. The more the merrier! Come, everyone is in the drawing room. Let's be seated. The servants will serve us tea and there is plenty of freshly baked apple torte. We shall discuss the most recent news and perhaps, even some gossip," said General Repin.

The servants entered the room carrying platters of food. Princess Cassandra could not help, but be charmed by a young girl who was carrying a platter of *zakuski* (appetizers). The servant reminded her of her own daughters, Maria and Smaragda.

"What a lovely girl. She has a sweet demeanor," said Cassandra, watching the girl as she placed the platter in the center of a long dining table.

"That is Lovisa von Burghausen, a Swedish girl, taken captive during the war. I am very fond of her. She is a hard worker and dependable," replied Princess Prascovia.

Lovisa kept silent. She knew her place and did not dare to look up at the guests. She did not want to offend her master for fear of being sold again.

"Oh, how unfortunate," replied Cassandra.

"Yes, but she is treated well and I consider her part of the family," answered Princess Prascovia.

"That is important. One should not be taken for granted, if even a servant. Princess Prascovia, before we continued our talks, I have a gift for you," said Cassandra, handing the Princess a small gold box.

Princess Prascovia placed the box on her lap and untied the blue ribbon that was wrapped around it, opening it carefully. "How exquisite, a diamond brooch! It's breathtaking. What a wonderful memento, but I have nothing in comparison to return," she said, looking up at Lovisa as the girl poured more tea. "Lovisa, come here. Since Princess Cassandra has taken such a liking to you, I have decided you belong to her now."

Princess Cassandra and Lovisa exchanged glances. Smaragda and Maria giggled at the thought of a servant girl their age in the household. They had a new playmate and they were in high spirits thinking of all the mischievous adventures that would include her.

It was a grand time at the Black Dirt estate. The Kantemir children ran and played among the grounds of the many blooming fruit trees on their estate. The same fruit trees, once so familiar in another country, not so long ago made them feel at ease in this new land. Lovisa joined the children in their activities when she was not busy attending to the household chores of the day. She was a foreigner in this country, as were the Kantemirs. She quickly adapted to her new life with them and became a valuable member of the household. It was spring and Chornaya Graz had its own beauty and appeal. The leaves on the fruit trees had blossomed to shades of pink and yellow. The meadow grass turned from yellow to jade green, thanks to the rain from the previous month. Colorful vivid flowers sprouted on the grounds throughout the estate. Even though it was spring, a cool brisk wind had set in from the North. It was too cold to play outdoors. Today, the children occupied themselves in the large indoors, busy at their studies and occasionally taking a break to play and run about all the rooms of their vast stately home.

"Maria, come find me," yelled little Antioch. He was the mischievous one and for the moment had deviated from his studies. He pleaded with Maria to play a game of hide and seek. Being the youngest, he was Maria's favorite. She had missed Antioch terribly when she was away on a concert tour and she was only too happy to oblige him in whatever way she could when she was home.

Antioch knew exactly where to hide. He would look for a place where his sister would never find him. He would hide in the drawing room, a room with beautiful opulent furniture.

At times, he was even afraid of this room, as it was grand and overwhelming. The furniture often seemed to be glaring at him when he was alone, however, at the moment he would not let his imagination take over. The room was a perfect place to hide, and being a clever four-year-old, he thought the ideal place would be in the bottom drawer of the serving buffet. Maria would never find him there.

Antioch dashed into the drawing room as fast as his little legs would carry him. Unexpectedly, he tripped and fell. He was so flushed with excitement that he picked himself up and started to run again, but not without first glancing back to see what caused his fall. There was his mother lying on the floor.

"Mother, mother!" cried Antioch as he ran back to her. His body trembled and he began to cry uncontrollably. Somehow he knew the cries and pleading words for his mother to wake-up would not help. Cassandra Cantacuzenes did not move. She did not hear anything. She lay very still. "Papa, papa, come quick," screamed Antioch. "Something is wrong with mother!"

Dmitri and the servants rushed into the drawing room. Dmitri picked up Cassandra in his arms. He carried her to the divan, but it was too late. Cassandra had never recovered from leaving her beloved Moldavia as she had been weak since their move to Russia. The bitter rainy season did not help and now the cold and weather. She had spent time in exile in Istanbul with Dmitri, and later she returned to Moldavia and now Russia. She did not have the strength to start a new life in a strange land. The many moves took a physical toll on Cassandra and she was too weak to carry on.

What would Dmitri do now? What could he do? He had lost more than he could have ever imaged. He felt responsible for any consequences caused by accepting the Czar's offer to find refuge, even though there had been no choice. He had six children who depended on him and must make life as comfortable and normal as he could for them. Shaken, sad, and full of grief, he made the final arrangements for his wife.

May 11, 1713. Cassandra's funeral day began with a prayer for the departed. "Oh God of all spirits and flesh, who had trampled down death and overthrown the devil, do the same O Lord for thou departed servant Cassandra, in a place of repose, a place of verdure, a place of brightness, a place hence all sorrow, sickness, and sighing has fled away. Forgive Cassandra for any transgression which she may have committed, whether by word, thought or deed, for thou art a good God who loves mankind, for there is no man that livest and sins not, for only thou art without sin and thou righteousness is for eternity. Dear Lord, please bless Cassandra and have mercy on her soul."

Byzantine liturgy music from the choir filled the *Church of Our Lady Life-giving Spring.* A white casket, covered with purple and white tulips, was placed in a shiny mahogany carriage that was enclosed by glass windows. Reflections of water from the nearby pond sparkled off the gold insignia of *"K"* imprinted on the side of the carriage doors.

Prince Dmitri and his children stood behind the carriage. They walked in procession as the carriage began its journey to the island on the pond. Prince Antioch, his head up high, led the way. Although, he was the youngest, he had an authoritative presence beyond his years. Following from behind, his siblings, Prince Constantine, Prince Matvei, and Prince Sergei, their arms interlocked, briskly kept up the pace. Princess Maria and Princess Smaragda, accompanying their father on each side followed. They walked more slowly than the rest of the procession for Prince Dmitri was slumped against Maria's shoulder. He was weak from anguish, consumed in grief and struggling to support himself.

The procession passed the two gardens attached to the courts and along one of the three rays of alleys leading through the park. The entourage followed the carriage until it came to a complete stop. Ahead, calm waters of the estate pond greeted them. The casket was taken out of the carriage and carried onto a stair leading to the small island. In the center of the island, a rectangular hole had been dug out. Two men on each side of the burial site lowered the casket into the ground. The Orthodox priests swung their sensors around the casket and about the grounds, quietly reciting prays.

A gust of wind emerged from the pond's edge, causing the incense from the sensors to drift upwards. Spring leaves of ginger, yellow, and pink fell from the nearby trees and swirled around the mourning guests, floating gracefully downwards until they landed on the casket that had reached the bottom of its new resting place.

No one, except little Antioch, took notice of the six blossom leaves that had found their way to rest on the tulip-covered coffin. He knew not what, if anything, to think of it. He stared deep in thought. He keenly observed everything in his young age and kept a detail of it, a trait inherited from his father. Four booming cannon shots interrupted the serenity of his thoughts and signified the conclusion of the service. Two churchyard attendants took to their shovels and threw the soil of the earth on top of the casket. The soil fell slowly, as if caught in time; endlessly making its way down, covering the six blossoms with its brown warmth.

Princess Cassandra Cantacuzene, member of the Cantacuzene family, daughter of Serban Cantacuzene, grand duke and ruler of Wallachia and descendant of Byzantine Emperor Ioan VI Cantacuzene (1347-1354) joined her ancestors in the sunset of her thirty-first year.

Weeks passed. The family was in deep sorrow mourning their loss. With Cassandra gone, no one was running the household. There was no mistress of the house, nor did anyone pay attention to Lovisa. The ambitious wife of the baker of the Kantemir household, Duscha, took it upon herself to take charge. She was jealous of Lovisa's position in the Kantemir family and wanted the position for her daughter.

She would take advantage of this opportunity. Seeing Lovisa's plate on the table in the servant's quarters, she slipped some poison into her meal. In her sullen mood, Lovisa was oblivious that anything was out of the ordinary and ate quietly in the servant's quarters of the mansion. She kept to herself after Cassandra's death. She missed the lady of the house who treated her equally as she did her own daughters Smaragda and Maria. She ate slowly, poking her food with her fork, recalling her first introduction to Cassandra.

In a matter of minutes, Lovisa lost consciousness and fell to the floor.

A cool touch on her forehead revived Lovisa. She opened her eyes to see Princess Maria leaning over her and smoothing a damp cloth on her pale face. Lovisa looked around and recognized the massive bed she lay in as Maria's. The draperies of the canopy bed were pulled open and an assortment of pillows were scattered about. Lovisa felt content knowing that in Maria's hands, she would be properly taken care of. She closed her eyes and dozed off until a sudden jolt of pain from her throbbing stomach awoke her. She soothed the area with her hand hoping the pain would subside, but it did not help.

"It must have been that lamb you ate for dinner a few days ago. Our trusted doctor was able to find an antidote for your ailment. I believe he has saved you. The pain should be gone in a few days," said Maria.

"I am most grateful, mistress. When I am feeling better in a few days, I shall be up and about chasing you. You wait!" replied Lovisa in a weak voice.

It was not much later when Lovisa recovered from her illness that she overheard an Armenian captain ask Dmitri to give him her as a wife. She did not want to leave the Kantemir family, but she did not want to take the chance to be given away again and she had no desire to become a wife. She would think of a plan to run away.

The next morning before dawn, when the entire household was still sleeping, Lovisa rose quietly from her bed. She dare not leave by the door. It was constructed of heavy wood and made a strange loud sound when it was opened. She would climb out the kitchen window that was left slightly ajar during the night to let in the fresh air. Lovisa carefully pushed the window open. She lifted up her long skirt and jumped to the ground. She ran as fast as she could and into the morning sunrise. She knew of an English merchant in the German quarter of Moscow. She would go there. He would give her refuge.

"Lovisa, what are you doing here?" asked Mr. Feeble. He was perplexed to find the young servant girl at his doorstep. Clearly, she had run away from her master. He would allow her to rest before he would report her.

"Please help, Mr. Feeble. I have nowhere to turn. I will be married off to a stranger, a captain from a ship. I will be taken away, beaten and never heard from again, maybe even thrown into the sea. I beseech you have mercy on me."

"My dear, I'm sure you are being melodramatic. You may stay here, but only for a short time. I shall not be an accomplice to illegal activities and harbor a servant belonging to another," replied Mr. Feeble.

"Thank you, I shall not stay long. I am so tired and just need to rest a bit. I am ever so grateful," replied Lovisa.

"You can rest there," said Mr. Feeble pointing to a small chair in the corner of the room.

Lovisa was so tired that she collapsed on the chair. She closed her eyes and immediately dozed off. Mr. Feeble did not waste any time. He immediately contacted the Russian police.

"Get up!"

Lovisa was startled to see two Russian police officers pulling her from her chair. "No, no. Leave me alone," she shouted out.

"You are under arrest. You will bear the consequences of your actions. We will return you to your owner," said the police. They chained her feet and hands. They hammered nails through her shoes to make it difficult for her to walk. She was placed in a carriage and taken back to the Kantemirs. Duscha, not happy to have Lovisa back in the household assigned her to wash clothes in a stone kitchen so cold, that her arms became covered with ice.

She would have frozen to death if it were not for Smaragda and Maria. They bribed the guard of the estate not to say a word and to help them fold her chains in cloth, to prevent it from giving any sound. At night they took Lovisa up to their bedchambers. There she was able to sleep in warmth.

"Maria and Smaragda, I must travel to St. Petersburg for business. Although, you are the mistresses of the house, in my absence I need a man in charge while I am gone. The household will be under the supervision of Captain Ivanov and his wife," said Dmitri.

"Yes, father," replied both sisters in unison.

Duscha, having overheard the conversation as she passed in the hall, silently rejoiced. During Dmitri's absence she would be rid of Lovisa for once and for all. At first, no one noticed Lovisa's absence. Her chains had been long removed with Maria's intercession and with a guarantee that she would not run away again. Duscha had taken Lovisa to the Russian slave market in Moscow and sold her.

"Where is Lovisa? I have not seen her for a few days," Maria said to Smaragda, who could only shrug her shoulders and reply, "I have not seen her either. I hope she did not run away again."

Maria walked to the library room. The door was open and she could see Captain Ivanov was hunched over, studying a map on the desk. "Captain Ivanov, have you seen Lovisa?" asked Maria.

"Ah, Princess Maria, what do you think?" he said pointing to the map. He was preoccupied with thoughts of planning a new route for the Czar's ships and her query did not register in his mind.

"Captain Ivanov, have you seen Lovisa?" repeated Maria.

"Oh, Lovisa gone, again? No child, I have not and I have no time to look for her. She is ill-behaved and I shall report her to your father when he returns." His attention returned to the map, his finger circling a pattern as he muttered to himself.

Maria did not know what to think. She would have to wait and hope that Lovisa would turn up. Father would not be pleased with the news that she had run away again after her promise not to. Weeks passed. Maria knew Lovisa was gone and this time would not be found.

A commotion at the entry door interrupted any further thoughts of the runaway servant. Father had returned.

"Father, you are home! We have missed you so. How was St. Petersburg? Did you bring any books for us?" Maria asked excitedly.

"Yes, books for everyone. I have science books, mathematics books, language books, and even poetry books. Where is the remainder of the family," inquired Dmitri.

"We are here," answered Antioch, as he opened the bag on the floor and began to pull out dozens of books.

"How was everything under Captain Ivanov's supervision?" asked Dmitri looking about.

"Lovisa has disappeared. She ran away again, father. We have not seen her since your departure," replied Antioch.

"Well, never mind. We shall not keep her against her will. We will let her be," said Dmitri. The children, excited with their new books, gave no further thought to the missing Lovisa.

The solace of the grounds at Chornaya Graz was an inspiration. The early morning chirping of birds and the floral splendor made the estate more beautiful through the years. With Cassandra gone, Dmitri immersed himself in his writings. He wished she was with him to share the beauty of the estate. He often visited the little island on the pond where she was buried. He sat on a stone bench overlooking her grave. The environment comforted him when he felt gloomy. The only noise was the rustle of the delicate foliage of the birch trees when the wind picked up. The calming, peaceful sounds inspired him, turning his thoughts, into stimulating words.

States go through periods of rise and fall, determined by the natural laws of the universe, he contemplated as he took his quill and began to write on paper, The theory applied to all aspects of life, being a concept from the philosophy of natural evolution.

Based on that hypothesis he theorized that the decline of the Ottoman Empire would be inevitable. He characterized the sultans and higher rank dignitaries, as he had known them. Vivid observations accompanied by comments followed descriptions of social and cultural customs which Prince Dmitri included in his manuscript, *History of the Growth and Decay of the Ottoman Empire*.

He wrote *Descripio Moldaviae*, describing his native Moldavia's geography, social and political history. He paralleled the narratives of historical facts and events with personal notes, anecdotes and stories. He devoted himself to intellectual activities. His merits as scholar and historian earned him the honor of membership in the Academy of Berlin.

Refugee status in Russia did not deter Dmitri from following events in Moldavia and Wallachia. There were rumors the Sultan wanted to avenge the betrayal at the *'Battle of the Prut.'* He had not forgotten that Prince Brancovan of Wallachia had switched loyalty between Peter the Great and the Ottomans. An indecisive ruler was not to be trusted. There were consequences to such actions.

"The Sultan does not forget. The Sultan would have his revenge." Those were the words Dmitri sent to Brancovan, who remained in Wallachia after the Battle of the Prut.

Warnings of death by the Sultan's hand did not deter Brancovan. He remained deaf to the counsel of friends and family. His riches and gold bought him many friends in the Sultan's court. He gave exquisite gifts to the Divan and the Vizers. There was no hurry to leave Wallachia as he had a comfortable and luxurious life. His riches would save him from the Sultan's wrath. He was a spiritual man, and his faith was unwavering. He founded the *Monastery of Hurez,* a masterpiece of architectural purity and balance that came to be known as the *Brancovenesc style.* The architectural design was a synthesis of Renaissance and Byzantine architecture, with rich sculptural detail containing religious compositions with murals and icons visible throughout. Brancovan's strong beliefs had guided him in the past and they would guide him now.

Today, Brancovan could not function properly. His youngest daughter lay feverishly ill in bed. He would not leave her alone in her final hours. He held her hand and began to read from a prayer book hoping they both would find some comfort in the inspiring words. As he read, her hand dropped from his and she interrupted with a plea.

"Father, you must flee. I sense something horrible. You and my brothers are not safe. You must leave at once. Unspeakable things will occur if you do not listen. I am afraid for you."

Unable to continue further, her head fell to the side as she uttered her last words: "Martyrdom."

11

The Beheading
of the Brancovan Family

Bucharest, Istanbul: March 22, 1714–August 26, 1714. Unwittingly and oblivious that anything was out of the ordinary, the servants unlocked the palace doors to the mysterious guest. Before the doors could be opened completely, twelve armed Solaks stormed in knocking over chairs and pushing aside anything that was in the way. They ran through the grand hallway, their black robes fluttering behind them.

The Solaks had studied the floor plan of the palace before their departure from Istanbul. They knew exactly where to go and what to do. They were ready and prepared. They knew the Sultan would not accept failure for they were especially chosen from the elite infantry of the Janessary to serve the Sultan for this mission. They moved swiftly and proceeded until they reached the throne room and kicked open the doors. There stood Brancovan, the *Prince of Gold*. A look of astonishment was frozen on his face and he was speechless. He dared not move, for there was no time to react.

"I am Moustafa Aga. You are under arrest!" A black cloth covered his face; only his glaring eyes were visible. He was a giant of a man and towered over the other Solaks. Moustafa Aga stood out from the rest. No one had ever seen his face. He was clearly in command. He moved quietly, and quickly. His words, struck sharply like the edge of a blade. *Mazil* (death) he hoarsely whispered as he threw the black veil of death over the shoulders of Brancovan.

Hearing the commotion, Brancovans's four sons came running from their rooms. They too had no time to react. They were herded into the main drawing room along with the remainder of Constantine Brancovan's family—his wife, his four sons, Constantine, Stefan, Radu Bassarab de Brancovan (who was married to Anna Cantemir, daughter of Prince Dmitri's older brother) and Matvei.

"We must find grand treasurer Enache Vacarescu. He has information that is needed to locate Brancovan's gold and riches before the Sultan deposes of him permanently," said Moustafa Aga.

In another part of the palace Vacarescu sat at his desk, deep in thought and absorbed in the financial affairs of Wallachia. There was to be another tax increase to offset the mounting and unexplained expenses of the Ottomans. How would another tax increase be proposed to the people? What could be done? He looked at the figures, reviewed them over and over again. Would there be no other solution? He was preoccupied and did not hear the disturbances in the hallway. A shadow darted across his desk and interrupted his thoughts. He looked up and was startled to see four black robed figures rushing towards him.

He was grabbed without a struggle. That was the way of the Solaks. They were fast and silent with their swift movements. *Surprise and Strike* was their mantra. Vacarescu joined the remainder of the Brancovan family. He knew their time had come. They tried to appease the Sultan with gold, riches, and extravagant gifts, but it did not help; it only prolonged the inevitable. They were doomed and he knew it. He dared not speak his thoughts to the Brancovan family members. Not only was he the grand treasurer, he was also a faithful and trusted family friend He did not want to increase their agony.

"Let us hurry, time is not to be wasted," said Moustafa Aga. He turned to Constantine Brancovan. You, Brancovan, are no longer the ruler of Wallachia. You are deposed. You have made the Sultan extremely angry. Your betrayal is unforgivable. You and your family are our prisoners."

There was no time to gather family belongings or necessities. Thrown together like wild animals, the Brancovan family was forced to leave the palace. Moustafa Aga was the last to exit. As he did, he noticed a dark shadow swaying back and forth in one of the corners of the hallway.

"What have we here?" he asked in a deep voice. He pulled his sword from under his caftan. The blade glittered brightly in the dim light as he poked the object with it. He crept forward for a closer look. Was it some small creature, a dog or cat perhaps?

"Well, it is a little boy. Perhaps, a future Brancovan," he said.

The child was curled up on the floor, trembling and crying softly. Constantine's wife leered at Moustafa Aga from the small group that was huddled together and dared to yell out, "Please, leave him alone! He is only three years old and has done nothing!"

"Oh, this must be your grandson, another Brancovan. I shall

take him along. The Sultan will be pleased," replied Moustafa Aga, as he pushed the little boy into the circle of Solaks.

Immediately and swiftly as they had come, the entire caravan of hostages and envoys set off for Istanbul, disappearing just as they had arrived; into the darkness of the night.

Istanbul, Fortress of Yedikule. Originally, built during the reign of John Tzimiskes, Yedikule Fortress was destroyed after the first fall of the city during the Fourth Crusade. John VI Cantacuzenes rebuilt it in 1350.

The fortress featured seven towers. Originally used as a treasury and later a state prison, it was now a home for executions, torture and mutilations. Agony and solitude were the companions of prisoners. Misery was only released in the bliss of death, for no one ever came out of Yedikule alive, including its most notable prisoner, the young Sultan Osman II, who had been executed in 1622.

A black stormy night greeted the Brancovan family as they reached the gates of Yedikule. The small group of hostages looked up at the tall towering fortress. Their shadows cast on Yedikule's walls, no longer looked human. Lightening illuminated the skies and as if on cue, the booming sound of thunder erupted as the double doors of the tower swung open. Rain began to beat down fiercely, as if to fight some unseen force. The long sides of the tower stretched upward, endlessly, as if reaching to beg for forgiveness — or were it arms pleading for rescue, clawing to escape a pit of horror. Four rectangular windows at the very top of the darken tower allowed only the lunar light of the moon to enter the forbidden area as bats flew through its endless, darken corridors. Spiders on cobwebs, spiders crawling on walls, were also looking for a way out, but for now they were the window coverings of this desolate place.

There was no escape, now or ever. An unknown energy swiftly pushed the Brancovan family inside. It was a bad omen. The fortress was dark, bleak and cold. The smell of musk and dampness was over powering and the air was stale with the smell of blood. Water trickled from the gray stoned walls, forming small puddles along the broken cobblestones. The only light was from the torch of the guard leading the way. In procession, the family huddled together as one to keep warm as they followed the Solaks behind the guard. Another two Solaks followed the prisoners from behind. Their pounding footsteps caused puddles of water to splash up against the walls. The Brancovan family was led from one corridor to the next, an endless walk through a maze of corridors, each becoming narrower and narrower. They stumbled when they reached the last corridor; so narrow they had to squeeze through one by one until they reached a wooden arched door.

"Stop, I shall unlock the door," exclaimed a voice coming from nowhere. A pallid face that had not seen light for ages was attached to a raggedy figure that materialized as if from the decayed wood door that stood before the entourage. The figure holding a chain of keys used the largest one to unlock the heavy door of the main marble tower. The door made a loud lingering squeak as it was pushed open by two Solaks.

"This is your new home," the ragged keeper said, as he held a torch up high to expose a filthy room containing layers of straw that lined the stone floor.

"These are your sleeping quarters. They are just as comfortable as the ones in your palace. You will find it the most pleasing room in Yedikule after you have had a chance to visit the others," he smirked.

The Brancovans did not acknowledge his remark. They were too exhausted from the long journey from Wallachia. One by one they fell on the straw too tired to think of the present, and too afraid to think of the future. It would be there in the towers of Yedikule they would wait and have their fate sealed.

There was no hurry. Time was of no essence.

Topkapi Palace, Istanbul. "Have my prisoners arrived?" inquired Sultan Ahmed III when he saw Moustafa Aga enter the Audience Chamber of the palace.

Moustafa Aga's long fast strides caused the back of his black robe to make a deep sweep into the air. His face was wrapped in a black cloth. Not even the Sultan had ever seen his face. It was not important and it did not matter. Moustafa Aga never failed the Sultan. Today, he had glorious news. It would be a grand day and he would be richly rewarded, but most importantly he had accomplished an almost impossible feat.

The Sultan was sitting on his gilded throne. It was covered with embroidery and encrusted with gems and pearls. He had been impatiently waiting for this meeting with the leader of the Solaks. Unconsciously, his fingers tapped the arm of the throne. It was the moment he had been waiting for, for treachery would now be avenged. He had special plans for Constantine Brancovan and his family—plans that were known only to himself and no other.

"Let us continue our talks near the fountain," said the Sultan as he rose from his throne. "We must be discreet. The fountain noise will prevent others from hearing. Prince Brancovan still has many friends in the court. They are unaware of his capture and I don't want anyone to learn that he and his family are our prisoners in Yedikule. The moment is not right."

They moved to the small fountain at the entrance of the building, which dated from the 15th century. The crystal blue waters of the fountain sparkled in the morning sunshine. They splashed downwards into the basin making a sonorous soft sound. No one would ever image a sinister plot was unfolding among all the serenity and beauty.

"I have been thinking of an appropriate punishment, but don't want it executed just yet," whispered the Sultan as he stood next to Moustafa Aga.

"Constantine Brancovan will be first. That is all I call tell you. I shall give him time to enjoy the comforts of the tower. I shall give him time to think. Time is his enemy and when his time is up I shall be there," said the Sultan. "I will personally preside for time is on my side. There is no hurry, Moustafa Aga. Now, I shall give you your fee, so well deserved. You have earned your reputation as the fearless leader of the Solaks."

He handed Moustafa Aga a heavy bag of gold coins. Moustafa Aga reached out from underneath his black cloak and took the bag without saying a word. He rarely spoke, finding words inconvenient. Silence was his faithful friend. He let others speak. Through their words, he would find their weaknesses and when needed, he would act. That is what made him a great Solak—silence and patience allowed him to entrap the enemy.

"You may go. Your services are completed and no longer needed. You have served your Sultan well."

Moustafa Aga swept up his cloak with one arm and left the Audience Chamber of the palace silently and swiftly. The silhouette of his shadow was the only evidence of an audience with the Sultan.

Yudikule Fortress—June 1714. Three months had passed since the Brancovan family was imprisoned and held captive. Elegant clothing became rags of riches, coiffure hair became long and matted, and straws for bedding replaced ornate furniture. Bread and water were elaborate meals. Rats replaced dignitaries as guests for dinner. Food was delivered to the prisoners through a tiny bottom square of the tower room door,

The Beheading of the Brancovan Family | 87

which opened and closed briskly or not at all. Distant screams of pain from nearby chambers within the fortress walls were the Brancovans only companion in the dark and musty chamber.

Time passed slowly. Days turned into months. There was ample time for contemplation and reflection. The Brancovan's murky cell became a cubical sphere of celestial thoughts. Apprehension, uncertainty and anxiety of the unknown began to take a toll on its inhabitants. Were they never to leave? Have they been forgotten? Were they never to see the outside world again and to finish out their lives at Yudikule? Would they become like the ragged keeper who greeted them at the wooden arched door—a faceless shell of a person. Or would a death sentence be bestowed upon them? Would they have the courage for a quick death? It would be a relief from this pit of darkness, an unmerciful endless fall from the deepest depths of insanity.

Little did the Brancovan family know that the Sultan had not forgotten them. In fact, an evil plan was waiting to be executed.

It was another dreary day in the fortress and the Brancovan family was scattered about their prison room. Some were sleeping and some were praying. Their attention shifted when they heard the sound of the small square opening at the bottom of their door being burst open. Brown dirty arms pushed in plates of stale bread and a bucket full of foul water.

Constantine Brancovan had just enough time to reach out and pull in their meal when the door slammed shut, knocking over the bucket of water on the stone floor.

"Grandfather, we have nothing to drink. I am thirsty," cried three-year-old Ghregorie.

"Be strong, little man. It is only for one day and tomorrow we shall have more. Let us be thankful we have bread to eat," replied Brancovan. He took the bread from the dirty plate and tore it in pieces to distribute among the family members. It would be their only meal of the day.

"Let us thank the Lord," said the eldest son, Constantine, who was named after his father. He led the family in prayer before beginning their sparse meal. Thick silence loomed through the chamber room as the hostages ate their cherished bread.

"I will tell you a story you have not heard before," said Stefan the second son, trying to lighten up the mood for little Ghregorie.

"Be quiet Stefan. We do not want to hear your stories. We are miserable and nothing you say will help. What are we to do? We are finished. I don't care what you say. I don't want to hear anything. I need to get a message to my wife, Anna Cantemir in Wallachia. She was away visiting her family and does not know what has become of me. I want her to know she needs to go on with her life if I do not survive this ordeal. The children must not forget their father," interrupted a nervous Radu.

"Now is not the time to argue. You need not be so dire. You will dishearten the others. We need to be strong. Nothing will happen to us. We have done nothing to provoke Sultan Ahmed III. You are upsetting little Ghregorie," said the youngest Matvei. "He is already scared and your bickering does not help. What kind of example are you showing him?"

Ghregorie looked up at Matvei. He was lying with his small head on Brancovan's lap. He did not know what was happening and he was confused by his gloomy new home. He was hungry and cold. He snuggled closer to his grandfather to keep warm. Feeling content he drifted off to sleep.

At this very moment, Sultan Ahmed III had made a decision. He would confront Constantine Brancovan about his betrayal.

The guards in the fortress were scrambling about. The Sultan was here to see his important prisoner. They did not want to keep him waiting. Constantine Brancovan was to be fetched immediately. The Sultan would see him in a special fortress chamber, especially reserved for interrogating notable prisoners.

"Constantine, get out and follow us. You have a visitor waiting for you," said the guard as he opened the door.

"Grandfather, grandfather, don't go, you won't come back. I'm afraid," shouted a startled Ghregorie.

Brancovan picked Ghregorie up from his lap and gently stroked his fine brown hair with his long bony fingers. "Don't be afraid my little one. I'll be back. It is not my time."

Brancovan followed the guard through the twists and turns of dark endless passages. They walked until they reached the end of the last corridor and to a smaller tower. There in the center of the great chamber room, stood Sultan Ahmed. A white turban topped with a diamond encrusted palm leaf signifying victory and triumph was wrapped around his head. He wore a long brown fur lined green satin cape. A robe visible underneath was covered with rows of diamonds that matched his large black onyx and pearl covered wide belt. The black onyx held mystical powers that sharpen the wit and kept emotions and passions under control.

The Sultan had great confidence when he wore it, for the wide opulent belt had a large buckle compartment that held a hidden jeweled dagger should an urgent situation arise. The belt was the sultan's favorite and he wore it at all times. A yatagan *(Turkish sword)* with a single edge blade and a handle made of ivory with imprinted gold scrolls hung from the belt. Gold curled up shoes stuck out from beneath his robe and completed the ensemble. On each hand he wore an oval ring. The ring on the right hand contained a poison, the ring on the left, an aphrodisiac. He was always prepared for the unforeseen. The Sultan pointed his jeweled scepter at Constantine and in a stern voice began his lecture.

"I have given you enough time to think of the consequences of your betrayal. Are you ready to confess your disloyalty? I know that you contacted the Czar of Russia during the war and accepted gifts from him instead of supporting me. You gathered your troops in Urlati, near Moldavia, to offer your services to the Czar and yet, you changed your mind at the last moment in my favor. How can I trust you again? Is it because you sensed a Russian loss and a Turkish victory that you changed sides? Though, you returned the gifts to Peter the Great, you are no longer trustworthy and you have no loyalty. You are not a man and therefore, not qualified to rule any people. There is no room in my kingdom or any other for such treason."

Constantine looked at Sultan Ahmed. He shuddered as their eyes met for he knew an unimaginable and unthinkable evil had come to life before him. His face was sullen. He had nothing to say. He knew no matter what was said, the situation was hopeless not only for himself, but for his family as well. He stood motionless.

"You are silent Constantine. Go back to your tower and think again. I shall have another audience with you in two months. Maybe, you'll be ready to speak to me then," said the Sultan.

A loud roar was heard as a black stonewall behind the Sultan divided in half and rolled open. A portion of the cobbled stoned ground where the Sultan stood, suddenly and without warning glided back into the wall and disappeared with the Sultan.

Prince Brancovan, took a deep breath, relieved he was spared—for the moment.

August 26, 1714. "Today is the day. I have decided to put an end to all this treachery. I will not let deceitfulness exist any longer," shouted the Sultan. "You, Bostandjibachi will join me and be present during the executions. It is the only way to regain my honor and the respect of my people and country. They need to know what happens to traitors of the Sultan. Let the Brancovans be an example!"

"Sultan Ahmed, I respect your wishes. However, I cannot be a witness and partake in your plan. I shall not be part of such atrocities. I have received many benefits from the Brancovans. They have treated me well. I cannot do such a thing. Please allow me to leave."

"No. You must be there. I demand it, unless you want to join them in their final hours," replied the Sultan.

Bostandjibachi, having no choice but to obey the order, reluctantly followed the Sultan to the tower. They walked through dark and seemingly endless passages that led to the execution room. The Sultan entered first. After taking a few steps he abruptly stopped, as if to deliberate and in a deep commanding voice gave his orders.

"Bring in all the male Brancovans and treasurer Vacarescu, too."

The guards dragged in the elder Constantine Brancovan, his four sons, Constantine, Stefan, Radu, Matvei and treasurer Vacarescu. The last guard carried petrified little Gheorgie.

"No, no," screamed Gheorgie.

The Sultan was deaf to the cries of an innocent child. He was stoned faced and showed no emotion as he stood in the center of the execution room. He would take control. This was not the first execution he had ordered and will witness, nor would it be the last.

Bostandjibachi could not bear it. He could not face Constantine Brancovan. He turned away and walked over to the far end of the room, just as the Sultan gave his order.

"You, Constantine Brancovan were silent when we last spoke. I shall begin with you first and I shall be silent to your cries and the cries of yours."

As if on cue, the executioner walked over and in savage cruelty grabbed the elder Brancovan by his thinning gray hair, throwing his thin rail body against the tower wall. Constantine's face hit the wall with such great force that the bones in his face splintered into pieces.

"Ah," groaned Brancovan as he staggered, trying to pull himself up from the ground.

The executioner took giant strides towards him and picked him up, holding him two inches off the ground. He was no more than a puppet with a grossly distorted face. Ready to throw him against the wall once more, the words of the Sultan halted the executioner.

"Stop, put him down! Constantine I am not finished with you yet! I will not let your suffering end so easily. You will witness the destruction of all your sons. It is only appropriate that I begin with your eldest son, your namesake. Guards, bring forth his son, Constantine," ordered the Sultan.

The guards dragged the firstborn by his feet and threw him head first onto a block of wood in the center of the room.

"Father, father!" he screamed.

In an instant flash, the executioner's blade came down. A jet stream of blood covered the wall. Brancovan's cries were faint with anguish when he saw his son beheaded. Bostandjibachi vomited at the sight, little Gregorie fainted. The executioner scooped up the head and threw it into the "well of blood," an opening in the ground.

"Bring me the second son, Stefan. It will not end here!" shouted the Sultan.

"Do not touch me. I shall walk on my own," Stefan said bravely. He did not wish to have his father tormented further

The Beheading of the Brancovan Family | 93

with cries of terror from his sons. He made the sign of the cross and addressed the executioner.

"Do what you must. My destiny is in the hands of another higher power, as is yours," he whispered to the executioner as he placed his head on the block.

The executioner, surprised by this unforeseen reply, jumped back with fright. No prisoner had ever spoken to him in their final moment and with such composure. What was he to think? Was there a bright glow encompassing the prisoner? He was losing his mind with all the executions. That was the only explanation. He hesitated for a moment, not knowing what to do. He did not wish to continue the slaughter.

The Sultan was not pleased with the hesitation. He did not want any interruptions. He was getting impatient. The beheadings had to be completed as quickly as possible.

"What are you waiting for?" he shouted.

The executioner looked at the Sultan. *I must be imagining things,* he thought. He had no choice. He would not go against the Sultan's orders for it would be his head on the block instead of Stefan's.

"Do not despair, father! We will meet again in a better place," Stefan cried out as he turned his head to see tears of agony rolling down the face of an old man. Once again the blade came down, more swiftly this time to spare any mortal pain. That was the best the executioner could do. He took the head and placed it into the "well of blood," still shaken by Stefan's demeanor in the face of death.

"Constantine Brancovan, you have another chance. I will spare you and your remaining sons if you will admit your treason, tell me the location of your wealth and renounce your Christian beliefs," continued the Sultan.

Constantine, weak with physical and mental pain, could not

and would not respond. Months of prayer and meditation in Yudikule Fortress had prepared him for this final moment. He was ready to meet his fate.

"Very well, then it is your command, not mine that I continue. Bring forth the next prisoner," he said.

Two guards dragged Radu Brancovan by his arms. Radu witnessed his two brother's beheadings before him. He would be strong. He prayed silently as his blood joined those of his brothers.

"Let us finish with the last son. I see Constantine Brancovan will not change his mind at any cost," said the Sultan.

The guards grabbed Matvei by his hair, throwing him forward onto the bloody block. Frozen with fear, Matvei was in a trance. He could not move and was unresponsive. He lay motionless as the executioner continued his work. Another spurt of blood covered the tower walls, spilling more unto the already blood saturated ground.

The Sultan was getting restless. Despite all that Constantine Brancovan witnessed, he could not be persuaded to admit betrayal and to renounce his faith. What was it that kept Brancovan so strong in his convictions during these horrific events? It was neither bravery nor valor. It was his passion, passion to cast out works of darkness, to put on an armor of light and strengthen the ascent of the heart to a higher source. His deep spirituality sustained him.

"Constantine, I will give you your last chance. I will spare your life if you admit your treason; denounce the beliefs of your homeland and of your ancestors," shouted an enraged Sultan.

Constantine was curled over on his knees for he could no longer stand. He lifted his head upward, oblivious to anything the Sultan might say and remained silent.

"Then, you give me no choice." The Sultan turned towards

treasurer Vacarescu. "I know Bancovan has an immense fortune. You are his treasurer. Disclose the locations of his wealth and I shall spare your life."

Vacarescu was overcome with fright. He could not move; he could not think or speak. He was paralyzed, knowing the inevitable was near. He knew disclosing any information would not spare him. The Sultan, seeing that nothing would be accomplished, said, "Constantine Brancovan, you have witnessed the consequences of treason. Do you have any last words?"

"If my death comes from God, as a punishment for my sins, His will be done. If it comes from my enemies, may Heaven forgive them," was Constantine's only response.

"Those words do not impress me. You will be united with the others in their fate," replied the Sultan.

Faithful grand treasurer Vacarescu and Prince Constantine Brancovan of Wallachia were then beheaded simultaneously. It was August 26, 1714, the sixtieth birthday of Constantine Brancovan.

"Ah," crying mad with terror, little Gregorie, the only male Brancovan remaining, ran aimlessly about. He stopped only when he reached the corner of the room and came upon the familiar face of Bostadjiibachi. He quickly scooped up the ends of Bostadjiibachi's caftan and hid underneath. Bostadjiibachi could only glance at the Sultan. He dared not speak. He took Gregorie from under his caftan, held him high in his arms and cast an imploring look at Sultan Ahmed.

"Could the Sultan be so cruel and without mercy as to take the life of a young child to compensate for the alleged sins of his grandfather?" he asked.

Sultan Ahmed looked at the petrified child. Satisfied that all treachery had been avenged, he made a sign of pardon. *I could be compassionate as well,* he thought satisfied with himself. Without a word, he turned his back on the bloody, soggy ground sprawled with corpses and walked out of the chamber of horror.

It was not long before the news of the Brancovan's family executions spread throughout Istanbul. The streets were lined with people who had rushed out to protest. They demanded confirmation or denial of what was rumored. Could what was alleged be true? The crowds began to grow and get louder. They lined the streets and marketplaces. They began to get restless in the hot sun, demanding that the Sultan appear and address the execution rumors.

"Ahmed! Ahmed!" the people shouted in unison. Before the Sultan could appear, the heads of the slaughtered family were carried on poles through the streets. The spectacle enraged the Muslim population for Constantine Brancovan was popular and a well-liked ally. Thunderous roars came from the crowd for Sultan Ahmed III to end this horrific display. For the first time, the Sultan feared a rebellion. He needed to think fast and act quickly, or he himself might become a prisoner in the tower of Yudikule.

"Take the heads back to Yedikule. Place them into separate bags and throw the heads and bodies into the Bosphorus," he ordered.

With the heads taken out of public view, the crowds began to disperse. They were satisfied that a stop had been put to the brutal display. Businesses of the day, haggling at the marketplace, buying and selling of goods, soon returned to normal. Occasionally, a whisper of the dreadful events of the day was heard. Life in Istanbul continued on as if nothing had happened. The shocking spectacle was forgotten by most, but not by all. A few faithful remained. They did not forget. When all calmed down, when evening became night, they made their way into their boats and sailed onto the gray mist covered sea. Sound of splashing oars echoed in the still of the night. Two boats, full of fishermen searched the darken waters. They held their torches high and then lowered them towards the waters. They were searching for bodies.

"Here," shouted one fisherman. "Here," shouted another.

Slowly and one by one, the bodies of the Brancovans were pulled from the Bosphorus and onto the boats. The fisherman did not stop until they found all the bodies, wrapping them in a white shroud cloth. It was sunrise when the grim task was completed. The boats sailed briskly on the Sea of Marmora, the morning skyline of Istanbul behind them. The waters of the sea splashed against the boats, splattering droplets onto the covered bodies that lay alongside one another. The sun's reflection off the glittering waters of the sea provided little clue to the horrors that lay within the vessels. They sailed rapidly, the winds pushing from behind, towards a small island that lay ahead. There, the fishermen buried Constantine Brancovan, his four sons and the faithful treasurer Vacarescu.

Bostandjiibachi had fulfilled his obligation to the Brancovan family. Little Gregorie was spared and taken under the wing of Bostandjiibachi for a safe return to Wallachia.

The "well of blood" long dried, but the horrors at Yudikule Fortress were not forgotten. (The Brancovans were eventually made saints of the Orthodox Church).

During the darkest times of life, solace can be found in the expression of words. Such words, written by my brother Benjamin Karanowytsch in New Britain, Connecticut, in 1963 expressed the sorrow felt by the fate of the Brancovans:

In Search of the Midnight Soul

On a quiet sea of air
Toward the heavens I'll calmly sail
And search for the midnight of the soul
The sands of time are sinking
There to an ocean of fullness
Onward search, for the midnight of the soul
The streams of earth I've tasted
The deep sweet well of love,
But, more deeply I'll drink above
In search of the midnight of the soul
Dark has been the midnight
Now the dawns of heaven breaks
The fair sweet morn awakes
To bring a new spring day at hand
With the web of time I weave
In search of the midnight of the soul

12

The Building of St. Petersburg

St. Petersburg, 1714. St. Petersburg was developing into a new and grand city. All nobility were encouraged to build homes and palaces. Peter the Great personally oversaw the construction of the city named after his patron saint, St. Peter the Apostle and made St. Petersburg the capital in 1712, moving it from Moscow. The focal point of the city was its first place of worship—the Trinity Church. Located in an area between the Peter Paul Fortress and the cabin of Peter the Great, it became known as Trinity Square. (*Troitskaia Ploschad*) Nearby was *Gostiny Dvora*, a market for local and visiting merchants, and several bars and inns. New construction of homes for the local nobility completed the neighborhood.

Prince Dmitri decided to have a palace built on a plot he purchased on the bank of the Neva River. It was to be built in a similar manner to his old stone palace in Istanbul, but with baroque influence, as was the fashion of the new St. Petersburg. He commissioned Francesco Bartolomeo Rastrelli, a descendant of an old Florentine family. Francesco's father was the prominent Italian architect Carlo Rastrelli. When Carlo Rastrelli was invited by Peter the Great to build the new St. Petersburg, Francesco came along. He had no formal training in the science and art of architecture, but saw this as a perfect opportunity to learn. The immense construction of St. Petersburg would allow him to work alongside side and match the talents of his well-known father. He was eager to begin, having spent much of his childhood in restricted Gothic Paris. St. Petersburg would provide the architectural freedom needed to incorporate both the traditions of European baroque and early Russian architecture.

Francesco Rastrelli's design began with a three-storied mansion with the main facade looking onto the Neva River. He wanted it to blend with the silhouette of the tightly built-up embankment. The auxiliary building would face Marble Street and the facade would face Millionnaya Street. The exteriors were to be decorated in baroque style with a wealth of decorative elements featured. Each design would be more elaborate than the one before. Added combinations of contrasting colors and mosaic finish would complement the great number of statues that were to be placed above the top exterior windows. The interior would feature flora motifs, beginning in the grand music room and leading to the gold lined double staircases. The building of Dmitri's Neva Palace would be a monument to his talent and would make the palace the first significant building in St. Petersburg. Fracesco Rastrelli would revive Russian architecture with his innovative ideas.

Dmitri was so satisfied with Rastrelli's plan that he asked him to design an architectural ensemble at his estate at Chornaya Graz outside of Moscow. Soon, Rastrelli's artistic architectural style became well known and greatly valued. His works caught the attention of Peter the Great and his daughter, Empress Elizabeth. They commissioned him to design numerous palaces, among them the Winter Palace (The Hermitage).

St. Petersburg became a city like no other. Academy of Sciences, a university where people would study medicine, philosophy and law was established. It would be "the assembly of the learned and skilled." It was a place for people who wished to obtain advanced degrees, as well as a cultural center and a place to handle strategic matters of state. In order to entice students, Peter the Great allocated 25,000 rubles per year to support the academy and promised to pay "healthy wages" to the academicians. Candidates to the academy were selected carefully and not all were admitted. They had to be exceptionally brilliant and young: the future of Russia.

The development of the Academy of Sciences posed one slight problem: There were not enough native scholars and foreign ones were not interested in traveling to the remote, uncivilized country called Russia. However, it was thought that once St. Petersburg was developed, foreign scholars would follow. Prince Dmitri assisted and provided his knowledge and skills as a scientist, writer, composer, philosopher, and a linguist, which proved to be valuable to the academy. One of the first students to attend the academy was Prince Antioch Kantemir. He was considered the most cultured young man in Russia at the age of eighteen and was admitted to the academy without question. He was educated in the arts and languages. Writing came naturally to him. His many satires and poems dwelling on the complexities of life earned him a reputation as a noted intellectual.

During the construction period of the St. Petersburg mansion, Dmitri concentrated on his writings. He wrote *Descriptio Moldaviae*, which dwelt with geography, social and the political history of his homeland of Moldavia with the idea of national independence and unity. It was the first completed geographical, ethnographic and economic description of the country. He drew the first real map of Moldavia. As Imperial Chancellor to Peter the Great and at his request, Dmitri translated the *History of the Growth and Decay of the Ottoman Empire* from Latin into Russian. He also wrote from a scientific perspective of his time in Istanbul and on the history of the Ottomans. Biographies of sultans, diplomatic statesmen and bishops of the Orthodox Church were included. It was the first work ever written on the mystifying land of the Ottomans. Dmitri accomplished all of this in one year. His brilliance for writing was only out shined by his talent for diplomacy. (Dmitri Kantemir's name is inscribed on a plaque at the Library of Sainte-Genevieve in Paris, next to Newton, Piron and other great minds.)

Today, Dmitri would take a much-needed break from his teaching and writings. "I must go and take a look at the progress of my palace. I want to see what Rastrelli has accomplished thus far," he said to his daughter, Maria. Dmitri could not help but smile when he looked at Maria's face. With her long chestnut colored hair and green eyes, Maria greatly resembled her mother.

"Father, don't forget; Rastrelli must design a beautiful music room in the palace. I will sing and play my harpsichord all day in such a fine room," she replied.

"Don't worry my sweetness. I have already arranged it. You will be pleasantly surprised. I shall inform you of the progress when I return."

Dmitri ordered his carriage and proceeded to the banks of the Neva River.

St. Petersburg of the early 1700's was originally a swampy, scarcely populated area. Now it was developing into a grand European capital. The Peter and Paul fortress, to protect the city from possible attacks by the Swedish military was almost completed. Across the Neva River from the fortress was the Admiralty. It was known as a shipbuilding complex and its vessels were to lead Russia to many naval victories. It housed the most powerful ships of the Baltic, which were built on the premises. It was one of the many preparations for war made by Peter the Great. During this time, and to keep abreast of the building of St. Petersburg, Peter lived in a small hut, known as the cabin of Peter the Great. He stayed there during the time the city was being developed and while waiting for the completion of his Summer Palace, which began in 1714.

Dmitri's carriage passed the Czar's cabin, but he did not pay attention for his eyes were focused towards the Neva River. The choppy rippling waters of the dark river appeared even darker against the low gray skies of St. Petersburg. Many boats were on the river, ferrying people between the banks of St. Petersburg. It was a sign that the city was beginning to prosper. Dmitri was so enthralled with the sight, that he did not notice the carriage was nearing his half-finished palace.

"Whoa!" exclaimed the coachman, an indication for the horses to slow their pace. Wanting to take a proper look and walk on foot the remainder of the way, Dmitri shouted, "Coachman, stop here. I have decided to get out and walk."

The carriage came to an abrupt halt. Prince Dmitri jumped out. His high black boots made sloshing sounds as they hit the damp ground. He walked briskly towards his palace, embedding his footprints in the muddy dirt along the way. "Slush, slush, slush," was all that could be heard as he continued his walk along the bank of the Neva River towards the palace. He did not notice the fast, darkened moving clouds. His eyes were fixed only on the three-storied mansion. He was anxious to see how much was completed on the exterior portion and in the interior music room as he had promised Maria he would give her all the details on his return. A light drizzle began as Dmitri approached the mansion. Fine raindrops fell on his face, but it did not matter, for he was highly pleased with the progress of the palace. Perhaps, it could be just a bit more ornate. He was deep in thought as he gazed upwards at one of the white stucco facade balconies.

"Oh!"

Dmitri's thoughts were abruptly interrupted. He had bumped into a person causing them to lose their footing and fall.

"Oh, pardon me!" he exclaimed. Embarrassed, he held out his arm to assist the fallen person from the wet ground. To his surprise, a disheveled young lady grabbed his arm and pulled herself up.

"My umbrella," she pointed out, as it rolled down the bank.

"Let me get it for you. It was my carelessness that caused all this."

Dmitri felt foolish as he ran after the umbrella. *What a spectacle I must be, chasing an umbrella in the rain,* he thought. He managed to quickly scoop up the umbrella just as it reached the river's edge. Dmitri swiftly climbed back up the embankment with umbrella in hand. By now, the drizzle had turned to a steady rain.

"I shall take care of any damages," he said as he returned the umbrella to its owner. He noticed the young lady trying to pull herself together. Her hair and dress became disheveled in the fall. Her feathered hat had slipped to one side, causing it to sit crooked on top of her head and her dress was wet and splattered with mud.

"What a sight I must be," she said as she adjusted her hat and looked down at her dress. "I must look dreadful," she continued as she tried to brush off the dirt and mud from her clothing.

She looked up at Dmitri. As their eyes met, this beautiful stranger immediately captivated him. Dmitri hesitated for a moment at this unexpected turn of events, not knowing what to say or what to do. Before he had any time to think, or worse yet, make a complete fool of himself she replied.

"Thank you, sir. It was not really your fault. The architect of this palace and the wonders of St. Petersburg dazzled me as well. The city is developing so beautifully. The Peter and Paul Fortress is spectacular and the Admiralty complex is just about completed. They say the most powerful Russian naval ships will be built there. The waterway between the banks gives the city a European flavor. I like that feature, for I was educated in Sweden. I welcome the European style of St. Petersburg, our 'Venice of the North,'" she stated as they walked arm in arm sharing the umbrella and up the bank.

"Let me introduce myself," said Dmitri, his senses returning and curious to the identity of this lovely young lady. He was pleasantly struck by the softness of her voice and her feminine ways reminded him of his beloved Cassandra.

"I am Prince Dmitri Kantemir. This is my palace."

"I am Princess Anastasia Ivanovna Trubetskaya," she replied.

"Here we are. Come inside and wait a moment. I must take a quick look around," continued Dmitri as they entered the palace.

The princess turned her head to glance at a room off the main entrance, its high ceilings lined with dozens of chandeliers. "Oh, this is lovely!" she exclaimed.

"That's the grand ballroom. Our family entertains quite often. Dignitaries, ambassadors, educators and even the Czar himself are guests during our balls and receptions," answered Dmitri.

"Really, entertainment was very much part of my social life during my time in Sweden," said Anastasia as they continued the tour of the palace.

"Look, Anastasia! That is the music room. It is being built especially for my daughter, Maria," interrupted Dmitri.

They both stopped to admire the large room on the opposite side of the grand ballroom. The music room was located next to the white marble gold lined double staircases that led to the upper floors. White and gold moldings with delicate intricate floral designs lined the walls of the music room.

"Yes, I do believe Maria will be happy with this room," said Dmitri.

"Oh, I believe I have heard of Princess Maria Kantemir's vocal talents. Very captivating, I'm told. I sing and play the piano myself, so I appreciate fine music."

"Thank you, but look at your clothes! We must take care of them. Your dress and cloak are still wet. You need some dry, clean clothes. I will have my coachman take you home," said Dmitri.

"Thank you again, sir. I accept on the condition that you stay for tea. I would be most pleased if you would be the first visitor to enjoy a cup of tea from my new silver samovar. I cannot think of a more worthy guest. It would do us good and warm us from the dampness of the day. I will have the servants prepare some jam, honey and a bit of *zakuski* (appetizers). I won't take no for an answer. You must accept," said the Princess.

"I will be most honored to accept such a tempting invitation from such a charming young lady. I also have one condition. That in the spring, you will be my guest at my estate Chornaya Graz, near Moscow, my main residence," continued Dmitri.

"I really shouldn't. I am not in the habit of accepting such invitations from strangers, but I have heard much about Prince Dmitri Kantemir, Imperial Chancellor to Peter the Great and his contributions to the establishment of St. Petersburg. I too, have a great interest in the development of St. Petersburg. You are no stranger to me. I accept your invitation," replied Princess Trubetskaya with a beguiling smile on her face.

"Wonderful! I shall close up. My coachman is waiting nearby." Dmitri took one more glimpse inside his almost completed mansion and locked the entry doors. He held out his arm to the Princess and she graciously accepted it, putting her arm through his.

"Coachman, take us to Princess Trubetskaya's residence," said Dmitri, as he assisted her into the carriage.

The carriage proceeded down the muddy road with the horses picking up speed, trotting briskly, causing the spinning wheels to splatter mud on nearby buildings as they passed. The roads were lonely and deserted. All was quiet except for the rain drops that beat steadily on the carriage windows. A symphony of thunder accompanied the horse drawn carriage with its lone occupants, down Millionnaya Street and out of sight.

Unknown to Dmitri, he would never live to see the completion of his palace on the Neva River. (The Neva Palace is currently the Russian Commercial Maritime offices.)

13

Easter at the New Estate

Spring 1716. Prince Dmitri, satisfied with the developments of his new palace in St. Petersburg, decided to return to Chornaya Graz to celebrate Easter. The entire Kantemir family would be waiting for him at the estate, to join the festivities on this occasion of Easter *(Pasha)*.

Originally a wasteland in 1589, Chornaya Graz had developed beautifully over the years. Rough terrains, multiple rivers and numerous picturesque ponds dominated the area. Fruit trees and greenhouses were spread throughout its land and forests. During the spring, it became an oasis as it unraveled from its hibernated winter cocoon state and wrapped itself in a cascade of vivid colors. Magnificent blooming tulips engulfed the gardens with their radiance. Sparkling crystal waters of the fountains echoed ever so softly in the distance. Statues, holding water spouted vases further decorated the grounds. Chirping birds with their exotic sounds kept harmony with the flowing waters of the fountains as they flew from tree to tree. Birch trees were scattered along the many streams of Chornaya Graz. Their swaying leaves rustled in the gentle breezes and joined in nature's choir of rustic sounds. Mixed wild flowers of yellow and blue sprouted throughout the estate. A wooden church, *Icon of Our Lady Life-Giving Spring* stood in the midst of this paradise. Chornaya Graz with its outdoor grandeur was a land only known in Russian fairy tales.

Princess Maria and Prince Antioch decided that a stroll through the gardens would lessen their anxiety of waiting for the arrival of their father.

"Before too long, father will be here. Let's take a walk and enjoy the fresh air," Maria said to Antioch, taking him by the hand.

They made their way to a small path that led to one of the many gardens and one of Maria's favorite, the luxurious rose and herb garden. She loved the greenery and the aroma of fresh thyme and basil along the path's edges. She breathed in the clean, crisp, pure and unfiltered air that lingered throughout the area. She stopped momentarily to gather some basil. Pulling a lavender colored ribbon from her hair, she used it to tie the basil in one bunch. She would bring it back to the main house and place it in a basket next to her white cast-iron tub. The aromatic fragrance would be most welcoming when taking a lingering evening bath. They made their way past the herb garden and on to the rose garden. The scent of roses filled the air. Maria would send the servants back, to gather some and set them in a vase next to the basin in her lavatory. The gardens had a calming effect on Maria. She came here when she was unsettled and needed to think. It was easy to become lost in the rapture of the tranquility of the gardens, its serenity unknown to most. The scent of roses soon became overshadowed by the dewy scent of greenery as they returned to the main house.

"We must hurry back, father will be arriving soon," said Maria. When they neared the house, they heard familiar voices, indulged in conversations of Greek, Moldavian and Russian. It was the Kantemir family custom to speak several languages among each other.

Today was going to be a special day for Prince Dmitri had asked Princess Trubetskaya to join him and his family during the celebration of Pasha. She was constantly on his mind since their first meeting on the banks of the Neva River. Spring in all its glory would be the perfect time for what he had in mind. He arranged a luncheon in his favorite garden, the one with the many tulips. All the tulips of his favorite color, white and lavender were in bloom. It reminded him of the tulips in the court of Sultan Ahmed III. Dmitri called him the Tulip Sultan. He could not help, but reminisce of his time in Istanbul, a time of intrigue, mystery and deception. It was his last dinner with the Sultan in Istanbul before his return to Moldavia that was on his mind as his carriage made its way down the long dirt road to the main residence of Chornaya Graz. It made him recall the carriage ride through the courtyards of the Sultan's palace in Istanbul so many years ago.

Topkapi Palace—Istanbul. The carriage approached the Imperial Gate of Topkapi Palace. Prince Dmitri gazed at the massive high arched gate with its gilded Ottoman calligraphy of verses from the Holy Koran.

Guards stood on each side of the gate. They were well trained in royal crests and insignia. They immediately recognized the regal crest of 'Kantemiroglu' and waved the carriage on. The guards stiffened with a grand salute as the carriage passed to the First Court. The First court, surrounded by high walls was filled with rose gardens, several fountains, and pavilions. It was paradise within a paradise. Prince Dmitri admired the lavish green grounds as his carriage passed the *Cinili Pavilion* that dated back to 1473. His royal carriage proceeded through the large *Gate of Salutation* with its two large octagonal pointed white towers. It led the way to the Second Court and to the palace. The carriage stopped when it entered the Second Court for many gazelles and colorful peacocks surrounded them.

"We have arrived, your sereneness," said the coachman.

Prince Dmitri climbed out of the carriage without replying. The footman handed him his tanbur and the prince started to walk the remainder of the way. The Sultan had granted him special permission to proceed through the 'Gate of Felicity' to the Third Court, a court that was in the private residential area of the palace. The gardens of the court were lush and adorned with lavender tulips, the Sultan's favorite. The fragrance of tulips, nature's freshener filled the air on this beautiful day. The prince was lost in his thoughts wanting to hold the moment in his mind. He would write about the wonders of these grounds. He continued his walk, through the splendor and grandeur of Topkapi Palace until he reached the Imperial Hall with its large dome. He noticed that the hall had classical paintings adorning the domed arch and the walls. He glanced across the hall to the Imperial throne.

It was empty for Sultan Ahmed III had not yet arrived, however, the Queen Mother and her consorts were all waiting. Members of the Dynasty, the *Hasseki* (the Sultan's first wife) had also arrived. The reception hall was crowded for many guests had come to pay homage to the great Dmitri Kantemiroglu. They were all standing, waiting, not daring to be seated until the Sultan arrived. Admiring glances greeted the Prince, but he too had to wait for the Sultan's appearance.

A hush fell over the noisy hall for the Sultan had entered through a secret door from behind a mirror, and then magically was seated on the golden ceremonial Bayram throne that was mounted with thousands of sparkling tourmaline. He had a long beard and wore a white turban on his head. Now the festivities were allowed to commence.

"My dear guests, today's feast is in honor of Prince Dmitri Constanovich Kantemiroglu. His great contributions to Turkish classical music is evident, his musical compositions and theories further beautify our unique culture. His intellect and knowledge of our great country is unparalleled. Let us all wish him the best on his departure. Hold your glasses high to toast him. *Salam-ala-kam*. Peace be with you Kantermiroglu."

"*Salam-ala-kam*," was echoed in the Imperial Hall as the guests repeated the salute, raising their wine-filled crystal glasses.

Smiling proudly, Dmitri replied, "Peace be with you as well."

"And now my honored friends, let's begin this grand evening. The Prince has graciously accepted my request to play the tanbur for one last time. Let's all be seated," said Sultan Ahmed III.

On that cue Prince Dmitri walked to the center of the massive room. The hall was silent with anticipation as he sat in a red satin, gold ornate chair. He took his tanbur in hand and began to play as his Greek music teachers had taught him. The music coming from the long necked lute reflected the innovative style of classical *peṣrev* and *ṣaz ṣemai*. His composition consisted of Ottoman melodic traditions with added tinges of European harmonic and Western overturns—a blend of European and oriental music. The beautiful melody and the glamour of Ottoman music played in Baroque style captivated the audience. They listened as if in a trance, for they never heard anything so sad, so sweet. Then, it was over, just as it began. The serene sound of music had come to a stop and returned all to reality from which place the melody had taken them. A few women remained misty eyed from the unforgettable whimsical song and that was the magic of Kantemiroglu's music.

"Saz Semai" in *Makam Neva* is dedicated to the great Sultan Ahmed III. Many years to you Sultan," proclaimed the prince.

"Thank you, my friend," replied the Sultan, overjoyed that such a beautiful piece was dedicated to him. "I shall always cherish the book of music compositions which you have graciously gifted me on the occasion of my ascension seven years ago. You bought musical culture to our empire by your note format of Turkish music. Your note marks enabled musicians to read and write our Ottoman music and not rely on memory any longer. Your music will be historical for Turkey and future generations. I personally thank you for your contribution in preserving our history, culture, and music. Let's all continue this evening with a specially prepared dinner for this memorable occasion."

Thousands of colorful tulips encircled the many rows of long tables that were lined with candelabras. Rare 14th century Longquan celadon Chinese porcelain from the palace kitchens were set in perfect order on the tables. The rare and precious wares dated from the late Song Dynasty (13th century) to the Ming Dynasty (1368-1644) and to the Qing Dynasty (1644). They were to change color if food or drink was contaminated with poison, however, on this occasion there was little thought of anything ominous.

The kitchen staff of 1,000 had prepared for days in the several buildings under the domes of Topkapi Palace. Hundreds of cooks, specializing in soup, pilafs, kebabs, vegetables, fish, bread, pastries and sausages indulged in the world of cooking for this special banquet. They dedicated their lives to the Sultan as his chefs. Only the best ingredients acquired from the Spice Road and under the strict standards established by the courts and under the control of the Sultan were used. The hunters, fishermen, kebab chefs, butchers, cheese makers, and yogurt merchants would not disappoint the Sultan and his guests. Their contributions would make this evening unforgettable. Several trays of roasted pigeon and stuffed melons were placed on each table. The omnipresence of culinary delights—pilaf, *dolma* in various forms, kebabs, all flooded the tables. A feast so elaborate it could only be compared to the holy month of Ramadan.

Prince Dmitri thought of his late wife, Princess Cassandra Cantacuzene, and vividly recalled how beautiful she was that evening, as she sat next to Sultan Ahmed. She had arrived earlier and separately from him. She wore an ivory taffeta gown, the puffed sleeves of the gown were in quarter length and a double row of pearls adorned both of her wrists. Another strand of pearls hung from her neck. Her soft brown hair cascaded along her creamy face, causing her olive colored eyes to appear iridescently green.

What an opalescent sight my wife was, he thought, remembering how she captivated the Sultan as well on that last night in Istanbul.

"Come, my dear and be seated next to the Sultan and myself," said Princess Cassandra. She took her husband by the hand and gave it a squeeze as he sat down. The Sultan's table was a glow with two large golden candle-holders, each weighing 105 pounds and mounted with 6666 cut diamonds.

"Your kitchen staff and guild of cooks have certainly outdone themselves this evening," said the prince.

"Yes, they have. The food is a mix of regional cuisines from across the empire. Let us all enjoy our last evening together. You will be busy in the next few days before your departure. Enjoy, for I'm sure you will never taste such delicacies in Moldavia," answered the Sultan.

The sound of the ceng, a type of a harp placed on the musician's knees interrupted their conversation. Several kucek dancers took the floor twirling in their white skirts, wearing matching conical caps on their heads. The kucek dancers were men however; they imitated girls in appearance and in demeanor. They danced to entertain the Sultan and his guests with their spectacular moves and turns. The prince and the sultan were quite amused. They agreed this was an event to remember. They reminisced of their early years and expressed amusement when speaking of times spent together. The feast continued until the early morning hours. Only the sound of chirping birds made them realize how fast the night had slipped by and that all the guests had departed.

"I have something to be remembered by both of you before we conclude," said Princess Cassandra. She had a surprise for the sultan and her husband. She had waited until after the banquet and now was the right moment.

She placed an object covered with a cloth on the clean white table linens, which earlier had been replaced by the servants. Her delicate white hands removed the cloth, revealing a brilliant silver gilded ewer and basin set decorated in ornate Northern Baroque style with floral designs, yet also covered by exotic shapes of Islamic objects. The coat of arms and initials of Ioan Serban Cantacuzene were inscribed on the exterior of the basin. It was made of 10 pounds of silver. The spout and the thin delicate handle of the ewer were in the shape of a serpent. The lid of the ewer was a gilded royal crown.

"This is part of the dowry given to me by my father, Serban Cantacuzene, duke and ruler of Wallachia on the occasion of our marriage in 1699. You both will wash your hands. The ewer's design of baroque signifies a new beginning for the prince; the Islamic objects reflect peace for the Sultan. Although, your destinies will take different paths, this ceremonial hand wash will unite you as brothers and bring your two worlds together," concluded Princess Cassandra.

The servants poured water from the ewer into the basin. The prince and the sultan washed their hands together for the first and last time, unknowing, that within a year, the prince would have to flee for his life into a new exile—and the Sultan would have the blood of an unforgivable sin on his hands; the executions of the Brancovans.

Dmitri's memories of his departed wife Cassandra, and of his time in Istanbul in the court of the Sultan, returned to the present day and to the impending question he would ask Princess Trubetskaya. As the carriage approached the main gate to his estate of Chornaya Graz he could see a figure walking towards him. The glare of the afternoon sun was in his eyes and he could barely make out the figure approaching him. Yes, it was Princess Trubetskaya. She was walking from the main house, along a path lined with rows of trees on each side. They had spent the last few months together and have gotten to know each other well. He had to let her know he was serious in his affections towards her. He could feel she felt the same and he would not waste time making her aware of his feelings.

"*Anaschka!* You have never looked lovelier!" exclaimed Dmitri, as she got closer. *Anaschka* was his affectionate name for the princess. He kissed her on each side of the cheek, three times, as was the custom.

"You are in deep thought. What is on your mind?" she inquired.

"Come, let us have lunch. I will say to you what has been on my mind," said Dmitri.

Dmitri took Princess Trubetskaya by her arm and they walked slowly to the rear of the house and to the garden where the remainder of the Kantemir family was gathering. Dmitri was smitten with Princess Trubetskaya. She wore a turquoise satin gown lined with gold trim. The bodice was low cut and exposed just the top of her breasts. Turquoise drop earrings surrounded by diamonds further accentuated her matching flowered diamond necklace.

The sunny blue skies were filled with white luminous clouds and the day could not be more perfect for an Easter feast. *Pasha,* derived from the Jewish word had the meaning of *passing with Christ to the other life.* Surely, this day would be filled with belief, hope and love. Beneath the birch trees and in the center of the garden, an elaborate long table was set up. White embroidered linen covered the elongated table. Lavender and white tulips in delicate porcelain white vases were lined atop the table.

Appetizers of various sorts, anchovies, herring, *blini,* cheese and delicate bowls of caviar crowded the table alongside brown Russian bread. Towering, overflowing red grapes hung from a nearby tall crystal bowl. Next to the table, ice filled silver buckets sat on silver stands containing cold bottles of vodka. Vodka complimented the caviar. It was a nice paring to the appetizers and would cool the palette on a warm afternoon.

Meat filled pastries, *piroshky* and *plemeni,* complimented the pastel colored Easter eggs that lay in laced covered baskets. The servants worked all night coloring the eggs in onion peel, producing a variety of red, yellow and brown hues. Easter eggs were the main symbolization of the resurrection. The eggs would bring a new essence, a new beginning to one's life on earth. They were always part of the *Pasha's* celebration. With this theme in mind, Dmitri chose *Pasha* as the ideal time to make a life offering to Princess Trubetskaya.

Dmitri pulled out a white satin chair with the golden crest of the letter "*K*" embroidered on the seat back for Princess Trubetskaya. She took her seat beneath the shaded birch tree. The sun shone behind her, giving her chestnut colored hair, a radiant glow. The princess sensed this was going to be an unforgettable moment. She admired Dmitri from the first day they met in the rain. Now, her admiration had turned to love. She had met many noble men who pursued her, but none that could compare to Dmitri.

Prince Dmitri picked up two crystal glasses and poured half a glass of red wine in each. The sun's reflection on the crystal glasses seemed to cast an illusion of floating red rubies.

"Christ is risen," said Dmitri, raising his glass.

"Indeed He is risen," answered Princess Trubetskaya, taking a sip of wine from her glass. "Let's indulge with some *Pasha* eggs." She reached towards a laced covered basket containing the various colored eggs. She choose a red egg and Dmitri followed taking the same color to exchange, a traditional custom originating from ancient times when Maria Magdalena came to Emperor Tiberius bringing him a red egg with the salutation of "Christ is Risen." The color red signified the color of blood on the cross that Christ shed for the atonement for the sins of mankind.

"A toast, my dear, may our love and mutual respect for each other be eternal. Now, I have something of great importance to ask you. You don't need to answer me immediately," said Dmitri as he leaned over and gave Princess Trubetskaya another kiss on her cheek. She smiled at Dmitri. She had anticipated this moment and she was confident there could only be one question he would ask of her and she did not need time for she was prepared.

"*Anaschka,*" Dmitri said affectionately. "It has been years that I have been alone. I have buried myself in my works without any thought for anything else, least thoughts of the heart. Then, you came along and a new world emerged. You made me feel alive again, in ways and in feelings that I thought I had forgotten. Would you grant me the great honor and share your life with me? I ask your hand in marriage. Would you be my wife?"

Princess Trubetskaya stood up from her chair. She was much younger than Dmitri and the same age as his eldest daughter, Maria, but she knew what she felt in her heart. She walked to Dmitri and answered, "I would be most happy to spend the rest of my life with you."

We will get married here, at Gornaya Graz. A special moment such as this can only take place at Chornaya Graz a piece of heaven on earth. Kantemirovka, the pergola on the round hill overlooking the pond is the ideal place for us to exchange our vows. I cannot think of any place more perfect," Dmitri said excitedly.

"Yes, I agree. Let us make arrangements for a winter wedding. It would be the most beautiful time of the year with a wonderland of hills and trees covered in snow," replied the princess.

"January 14 would be the perfect date after the New Year of 1717. We don't need to wait much longer than that as I have waited too long already. Come and let us have lunch and announce the good news to our family and friends, but first I have an extraordinary gift as a remembrance of my commitment to you," continued Dmitri. He reached into his cloak and took out a small gold box wrapped in a silver ribbon.

"This is for you, my love."

Princess Trubetskaya took the golden box and carefully unwrapped it.

"Oh, it's exquisite, a beautiful crystal Easter egg!"

She held the sparkling egg in her hand and moved it towards her face for a closer look.

"It's absolutely stunning!" she exclaimed.

"The egg was especially hand engraved and painted for you, my dearest. Look, it has a flat bottom and you can stand it on a desk or put it on your dressing table," said Dmitri.

"I shall put it on my dressing table, next to my bed. It will be the first thing I look at in the morning and the last thing I look at, at night. I will cherish it forever as it will remind me of your love and the wonderful memories of today."

"Look, there's Maria. My daughter will be the first we shall share our news with," stated Dmitri.

"Maria, Maria, come here and join us for a bite to eat. We also have good news to share with you," said Princess Trubetskaya.

"Dobreadyen, Princess Anastasia," said Maria acknowledging her. She then ran over and gave her father a hug, giggling ever so slightly.

"My, we are happy today," continued Princess Trubetskaya.

"Yes, I have some exciting news as well, but yours first," said Princess Maria.

"Maria, please take a seat," said Dmitri as he pulled out a chair for her.

As she sat down, Maria could not help, but admire the tulips on the table. She carefully pulled a lavender tulip out of its vase and held it to her nose. It had a soft aroma. Maria leaned back in her seat twirling the tulip in her hand.

"Maria, Princess Trubetskaya and I have decided to marry after the first of the year, here at Chornaya Graz. We want all our family and friends to participate and you my little one, are the first to know," said Dmitri.

"What a joyous occasion this Pasha brings today," replied Princess Maria as she jumped up from her seat.

As long as her father was happy, she would not interfere.

She knew her father's heart only belonged to her mother, Princess Cassandra. She also knew her father was lonely since her mother's passing. It would do her father good to have a loving wife by his side, even though she and Princess Trubetskaya were the same age. Maria understood the situation perfectly, for she had a similar surprise to divulge. She leaned over to give her future step mother a hug and then happily skipped to her father giving him an even bigger one.

"I congratulate the both of you. I too, have some news to share. You may have noticed the innocent flirtations between the Czar and me. You may be surprised as to what I have to say, but things have taken a new turn and I too have found love. As you know, I have performed for Czar Peter and his guests many times at his palace and he was greatly impressed each time I played the harpsichord. My sangria's during formal state dinners lighted the atmosphere and I know he enjoyed these performances because I could see it in his expression and I could feel it. Over time, I could not help, but notice that Czar Peter has displayed a great affection for me and I for him. However, for a number of reasons I hesitate to continue such a liaison. I am much younger than him, much like you father and Princess Trubetskaya Yet that does not concern me the most, for I have grown to love the Czar just as the princess has grown to love you.

There is Catherine, his wife. He complains about Empress Catherine for various reasons. He has spoken much to me about the situation and that confuses me even more. Czar Peter has made advances, which are hard to ignore any longer. I cannot think properly," continued Princess Maria.

"Maria, you cannot be wrong if you follow your heart. Czar Peter has spoken privately to me about you. He is fond of you and he is a great man. He has lost feelings for Catherine and she apparently as well for him. You have freshness and beauty and you might even one day be the future of Russia alongside of Czar Peter. He has mentioned he would push Catherine aside and marry you. He has no heir to the throne, only three living daughters out of twelve children. He wants desperately to have a son and he will not ask it from Catherine again. Follow your heart Maria and then follow my advice. Now, let's not talk about it any further, ask the servants to fetch the rest of our family so we may enjoy this feast," continued her father.

"There's Antioch! Antioch! Hurry; come look at the beautiful Pasha table. Delicious food and sweets await you," called out Maria as he approached the garden.

"Hrestos Voskrest, Christ is risen," said Antioch giving Maria a tender hug. Maria and Antioch held hands and joined the entire Kantemir family who had now gathered around the table.

"Antioch, before we begin to eat, recite the eulogy of St. Dimitrius of Thessaloika in Greek as I heard you are going to recite it for Peter the Great," said Maria

"No. The Czar will be the first to hear it and then and only then will I recite it for you, personally if you still insist," teased little Antioch.

"Yes, I just may have you do that," laughed Maria.

The Kantemir family spent the entire afternoon around the beautifully decorated table with its *Pasha's* delights and settling into the laziness of the day. It was a perfect setting to prolong and enjoy the warmth of faith and family at Chornaya Graz.

Not known to Prince Dmitri and Princess Maria, Empress Catherine had already noticed the spell Princess Maria had on her husband. Affections between Czar Peter and Maria would threaten Catherine's position. She knew that, however, what could she do? Peter was not one to be told what to do in matters of the heart as he had alliances in the past, yet Catherine never interfered. This would just pass, as had the others. If not, Catherine would take measures into her hands, but in the meantime, Catherine would wait and watch. She could not control the affections between Maria and her husband as they continued to develop deeper. She suspected, this alliance was different, more serious than all the others but she would be very cleaver. The right moment would come and she would not say a word until that moment arrived. Patience would be her guide and in time, her day would come. After all, she was still the wife of the great Czar and that had its advantages.

Summer, 1716. It was a warm summer night. A slight breeze rustling through the leaves of the birch trees provided the only relief from the heat. The blacken night sky had millions of sparkling stars that lit up what seemed to be an infinite universe. Princess Maria walked among the grounds of Chornya Graz.

Where does the cosmos begin? Where does it end? In centuries to come, will the stars still shine on the wonders of this earth, on these grounds? thought Maria as she stared above.

The stars looked down at her as she made her way to the carriage house. She had been invited to Peter's estate for he had asked her to play at a dinner event he was hosting. The carriage and coachman were waiting for her when she arrived at the stables. The coachman didn't need further instructions, as he knew well her destination and its purpose. Soon the carriage was on its way through the countryside.

Music could be heard as the horse and carriage neared the brightly lit palace of the Czar. Peter was having a small reception for his closest aides and friends. Most of the aristocracy had gathered; the Golitsyns, Romodanovsky, Dolgoruky and the Czar's must trusted aid, A.D. Menshikov and a few members of the Kantemir family. The carriage stopped at the main entrance of the palace. The coachman got out first and assisted Maria from the carriage. The double entry doors had already been opened by the servants who were anticipating her arrival.

Maria could see everyone was gathered and seated in the drawing room enjoying a drink of aperitif and were in light conversation. No one noticed Maria as she quietly entered the room and slid down at her seat at the harpsichord. She was dressed in a pale yellow summer gown with a triple strand of crystals around her neck to match the triple strand crystal bracelets around both of her wrists. It was as if she was a star herself, fallen from the heavens to play enchanting music for the earthlings below.

All conversations came to a halt as Maria began to play. All eyes were transfixed upon her, but none as much as Czar Peter's for he was intoxicated by her Greek beauty and her musical talents further tantalized him. He thought she was playing only for his ears, his heart and his soul and he became oblivious to anyone in the room. Princess Maria could feel Peter's eyes upon her. She became lost in the warmth of his intimate glances as she played. This was not the first time she noticed his eyes upon hers and felt his affection from across the room. It happened once before, although at the time she did not pay much attention. She recalled the first moment their eyes ever met at Chornaya Graz, when Peter first arrived as a guest of her father. It started with a first glance.

The Czar had come to discuss the latest developments of the Academy of Sciences in St. Petersburg and he had needed Prince Dmitri's additional advice as Imperial Chancellor as how to proceed.

Boom! Boom! Boom! The three loud knocks on the door sent the servants scrambling about. "He's here, he's here," whispered the servants among themselves.

"Come, come now. Let's not keep the Czar waiting. Please open the door and allow his highness to enter," said Dmitri.

One of the maidservants opened the door and immediately curtsied at the sight of the Czar. The maidservant dare not say a word as she looked up at her ruler. He was bigger than life, a giant of a man. She respected the Czar, but at the same time was petrified of him. She had heard many stories about Peter the Great and now he was before her. It was best she be quiet and kept her place. Without notice, Princess Maria stepped out from behind the maid and looked at the Czar, speechless for the moment. Czar Peter's startled eyes met hers and they both stood still. He felt his heart melting and for the first time in his life, he felt like a foolish little boy. How could such a young girl possibly have this effect on him?

"Ah, I see you two have met. Let me introduce you to my daughter," said Dmitri who was waiting at the entrance of the library. "My daughter, this is our Czar," said Dmitri.

"Your royal highness," replied Maria with a deep curtsy.

Czar Peter dare not let his feelings be shown. He acknowledged the princess with ever a slight nod of his head and continued to walk ahead. Each step he took produced a louder thump than the one before. The servants quickly moved aside, not to get in the way and to allow the Czar to proceed to the library, as it was the place where Dmitri did most of his writings. Peter entered the library, but not without first turning to take a look at the princess. Their eyes met once more just as the servants closed the double doors to the library room.

"I will love you until the day I die," breathed Maria.

The resonance of applause brought Maria back to reality. She had finished playing her piece at the harpsichord. The guests stood up and continued to applaud, but no one more loudly than the Czar.

"Bravo, bravo!" he shouted. Everyone followed the Czar's suit and joined in. "Bravo, bravo!"

Maria's face turned pink, blushing from the intimate glances from Peter and from the public display of approval that he initiated.

January 14, 1717. Spring turned into summer and summer turned into winter. The white and gray birch trees of Chornya Graz had icicles hanging from its many bare branches, the ponds were frozen and the grounds of Chornya Graz were completely covered in snow that glistened in the sunlight, casting off a brilliant sphere of colors. A frost had set in giving the estate the look of a winter wonderland, yet it was only when one spoke, that a bitter cold day was detected. Despite the cold, it was an unusual and beautiful day for a wedding.

Prince Dmitri and his children, Maria now seventeen, Smaragda sixteen, Constantine fourteen, Matvei thirteen, Sergei ten and Antioch nine years of age, were standing beneath the hillside pergola. The calm and quiet grounds near the pergola of Kantermirovka were decorated with rows of winter white roses and petals of soft pink lilies. Long satin gold and white ribbons hung from the top of the pergola. The slight sound of the wind swirling around the pergola was all the music that was needed for a glamorous and dramatic atmosphere of an outdoor wedding. The entire Kantemir family was attired in their finest furs to shield them from the winter's bitter cold. Taffeta gowns lined with chiffon and lace beading were visible from beneath the furs.

The pergola was lined with guests waiting for the bride. Princess Maria stood at the far end of the pergola. She wore a white mink jacket with a brown ruffled sable collar and matching cuffs, which accented her organza sable, trimmed skirt. She smiled when she glanced at her sister, Smaragda who stood beside her. Smaragda had an elegant mink jacket atop her gown, her hands kept warm in a matching mink muff that was decorated with pearls. The Kantemir brothers stood next to their sisters, attired in heavy long coats to keep out the bitter cold, the collars of their red silk shirts barely visible.

Peter the Great, one of the guests was a friend of Anastasia Trubetskaya's family and the union pleased him. He stood at the rear of the pergola not wanting to distract the importance of the wedding ceremony. Princess Anastasia at seventeen was the same age as Dmitri's eldest daughter Maria. Today, she would be marrying the former ruler of Moldavia and current Imperial Chancellor of Russia to Peter the Great.

Prince Dmitri stood impatiently at the entrance to the pergola, dressed in a full-length black mink coat. He was anxious for the ceremony to begin and just as he thought he could wait no longer, he saw Princess Trubetskaya on the path lined with pink lilies walking towards him. Two ladies-in-waiting walked behind her as she made her way to the pergola. She wore a luxurious white full-length mink coat. As the winter breeze picked up, an ivory chiffon dress trimmed with lace decorations fluttered from beneath her coat. Snowflakes from the naked branches of the white birch trees floated downwards, dancing in circles as the wind scattered them in all directions.

The princess neared the pergola, setting a romantic mood. Dmitri took a step forward to extend his arm. She took it and they stepped into the pergola as the ceremony of Holy matrimony was about to begin. Antioch stood to the side holding a blue velvet pillow with two golden rings atop. Taking the two rings, the priest made a sign of the cross over the heads of the bride and groom and began to recite.

"The servant of God, Dmitri is betrothed to the maid of God, Anastasia, in the name of the Father, of the Son, and of the Holy Spirit."

Anastasia put a ring on Dmitri's finger and Dmitri did the same symbolizing that together they are complete and perfect. They were handed candles to confirm their spiritual willingness to receive Christ who will bless them through the mystery of marriage. The right hand of the bride and groom were joined as one. The priest read a prayer, placing a crown over each signifying glory and honor with God. The couple was crowned King and Queen of their own small kingdom; their home being a domestic church for matrimony signified immeasurable self-sacrifice on both sides of the bride and groom. The service concluded with the reading of the Epistle and Gospel. The Gospel described a marriage at Cana of Galilee, that was attended and blessed by the Lord who converted water into wine. A common cup of wine was given to the couple to share in life's happiness and sorrow so that their joys be doubled and sorrows halved. Prince Dmitri and Princess Trubetskaya followed the priest in a circle around the table on which the Gospel and Cross were placed. They took their first steps as husband and wife, and as married couple, a circle in the center of life. A final blessing was bestowed upon them as they returned to their place at the altar.

"You are now united in marriage!" exclaimed the priest.

Prince Dmitri lifted the white lace veil from his wife's face. They exchanged kisses and hugs as they walked down the steps of the pergola. Shouts of congratulations from the excited wedding guests followed as pink and white lilies were thrown at the newly married couple. Princess Anastasia Trubetskaya stopped momentarily to pick a white lily and held it up, giving it a quick kiss and tossed it into the crowd. To her surprise, Princess Maria Kantemir caught the lily.

"You are next, my love. May happiness find its way to you as it has me," she said.

Princess Maria did not reply as she had other plans. Peter was expecting her for he too had left the ceremony earlier. She did not want to keep her sovereign waiting long. She took the lily and pinned it to her sable collar and made her way to the main house. The winter winds began to pick up, further scattering snowflakes about the excited guests who had scurried to their waiting carriages. They were to proceed to the manor and to the grand ballroom, which was already lit up with numerous candle chandeliers. Lively music welcomed the guests and promised an evening of spectacular food and entertaining. Enormous fresh flower arrangements were displayed throughout the interior and exterior frozen grounds of the estate. White lilies and pink roses formed a trellis over the entry door. Massive floral displays guided the way to the ballroom and to noisy conversations already under way.

"Antioch please, I ask you once more. Do not deny me the pleasure of hearing the eulogy you are preparing at the Slavonic—Greek—Latin Academy for the fall opening. We all are so anxious to get a sneak preview. Rumor is the Czar will be attending," said Princess Maria.

She smiled at Antioch who had already begun to walk to the center of the ballroom and began to state confidently to the wedding guests, "I have prepared a eulogy in Greek to Saint *'Dmitrius of Thessalonika.'* Yes, it is true Czar Peter will attend the Academy opening. The first reading will be for the Czar and for that very reason I am unable to recite it as my lovely sister Princess Maria requests. Disappointingly, I cannot oblige her request at this time however; I will be most delighted to recite it again after the Czar has heard it first."

"Well said, my little brother," answered Maria. Not all knew that it was Maria who had arranged the Czar to attend the opening of the academy. A secret she preferred to keep, as well as her relationship with the Czar.

"We shall await anxiously. Come, everyone, let's celebrate the marriage of my father, Prince Dmitri and Princess Anastasia Trubetskaya," she continued. She pushed the married couple forward as the musicians began to play a waltz.

Princess Trubetskaya and Dmitri whirled around the floor

and soon the entire crowd joined in. No sooner had the waltz finished that the music changed to a lively mazurka. This prompted the younger guests to join in. Music and laughter dominated the huge room. Princess Maria joined arms with the children and coaxed them to make a circle around Dmitri and his new bride. The groom picked up the bride by her waist and swirled her around in the center of the circle.

"Kiss. We want to see a kiss," echoed the crowd.

Prince Dmitri did not waste a moment. He ardently kissed his bride, causing the guests to roar with approval.

The moment was perfect for Princess Maria to slip away unnoticed. She would not be missed this evening among all the festivities. She had a more important guest to attend to. She quickly put on her white mink jacket and discreetly exited through a side door and into the snowy weather. She pulled the fur hood over her head to shield her face from the blowing wind. Her hands froze from the cold and she hastily slid them into her warm fur muff. The troika sleigh with three attached horses was waiting for her. The coachman helped her in and Maria covered herself with a fur throw that lay on the seat. The snow began to fall faster building up snowdrifts. They would have to depart immediately.

"Whoop, let's go," shouted the coachman as he tugged at the horse's reins. The horses jumped forward causing the bells on their necks to jiggle. Under darken skies, the sleigh with its lone occupant glided effortless through the ivory snow and to the Czar.

The wedding party and their guests continued to celebrate and enjoy the merriment of food and drink into the morning hours. They did not notice that nature's gift of falling snow had blanketed Chornaya Graz in a winter wonderland.

14

Winter Wonderland

The Czar was expecting her. He gave specific instructions for the servants to retire early as he did not want any interruptions. He wanted her all to himself. Soon Maria entered the bedchambers of Czar Peter. Her eyes had to adjust to the darkness in the room and her ears to the silence. She could see the fireplace in the far end of the room had been lit and was radiating with heat. It was the only light in the room. Two over-sized stuffed chairs were nearby, one on each side of the fireplace. A bottle and two empty glasses sat on a small table in between the chairs. The window coverings of the room were left open. The light from the snow-covered streets reflected off the windows casting a luminosity glow into the room. Maria glanced about. Was the room empty? Where was Peter? Before she had time to think or wonder any further, two strong arms grabbed her from behind, pulling her up from the ground and carrying her across the room to the bed.

"Peter, you are full of surprises," giggled Maria.

"Hush Maria, don't talk so much. You have been keeping your Czar waiting long enough." He placed her on the bed, kissing her and tugging at her mink jacket causing it to drop to the floor.

"Peter, don't be so impatient," laughed Maria. He did not listen and continued to pull down a strap from the top of her gown. Maria knew it was useless to reason with the Czar once he made up his mind. She helped him, pulling down the other strap causing the gown to fall, joining the jacket on the floor.

"I cannot take it any longer, Maria my love. Why do you torture me so with your innocence, your beauty, and your softness. Come stay besides me and make me worthy of your love."

"Your, royal highness, love cannot be rushed. I have waited for you since the first day I saw you in Moldavia, seated on your horse. You were so grand, so majestic. You did not notice me. I was but, a little girl in awe of an emperor. I have waited my entire life for you as I grew up and to be noticed by you. Please, excuse my impertinence your highness, I ask you to wait a moment longer. I have a small gift for you."

"My, little Moldavian princess, you are full of surprises and this pleases me," replied Peter.

"I have a memoir from my father's wedding. I want you to have it, a unique white lily—a symbol of our endless love," said Maria. She took the lily off her coat and placed it on the table next to the two empty glasses. "Hum, what is this? What a wonderful aroma, so sweet, an aperitif, perhaps?" she asked sniffing the bottle.

"Yes, my lovely *Maruschka* for later. You see, I can be a romantic too. I need not lilies or flowers. I need only you," he replied affectionately.

Exchanged glances, words were no longer needed or necessary. Maria lay down beside her sovereign. He took her in his arms and she could smell the freshness from his body. The smell of lavender soap lingered as he drew her near. He was not one for bathing or cleanliness, but he enjoyed his winter steam baths. She knew he had bathed especially for this occasion for today was not an ordinary day.

"Wait, Peter my love."

Princess Maria got up from the bed. She walked across the wooden floor in her bare feet. As she passed the fireplace, intricate shadows of light danced on her nude body creating an elegant and delicate work of art. Her long chestnut hair glistened on her back. Peter thought he had never seen anything so beautiful. He was mesmerized and he dared not say anything. He dared not move to break the enchanted spell that was cast, paralyzing him and giving him a feeling that he had never experienced. Was he hypnotized? There would never be such a moment again. He knew it. Surely, he thought Maria must sense and feel it too.

Maria took the lily from the table. She held it high in the air, twirling it and herself in a circle. She hummed softly, dancing to Peter, her hips swaying from side to side.

"My Czar, look, have you ever seen anything so beautiful?" she asked.

"Not, until tonight," he replied still star bound by her beauty.

"Well, my beloved. The lily is yours, as am I," said Maria as she threw the flower to Peter. He caught it with his rough hands.

"I have caught the lily and now I will catch you and make you mine," said Peter pulling Maria down towards him. The lily fell from the Czar's hand and slowly floated to the ground. Between the softness of overstuffed white down comforters, lost in love and lust, Maria and Peter sealed their love in the midst of a snowy Moscow winter night, stopping the hands of time for a moment.

The wedding reception at Chornaya Graz of Prince Dmitri Kantemir and Princess Anastasia Trubetskaya was the first of many balls, receptions, visits and entertainment. Princess Trubetskaya did not waste any time in organizing various events to which all the aristocracy were invited. Peter the Great who dropped in without announcement or formality frequented the home of the Kantemirs. It was on one such unexpected visit that caused Peter to witness an uncomfortable scene between Princesses Maria and her new stepmother, Anastasia Trubetskaya.

He had arrived at the estate to hear the sound of music coming from within. No one heard Peter's knock at the main entrance and he had to let himself in. The music guided him to the main drawing room. He opened the door to see Princess Anastasia playing the piano and joyfully singing aloud. Nearby, slumped deep in an armchair and expressionless was Maria. Instantly, the Czar knew the situation.

"Why, is it that only one talented lady is playing and singing? You Maria should not keep us from enjoying your talents. That is not the way to treat the Czar on his visit," said Peter glancing at Maria with a twinkle in his eye. He saw her eyes swell with tears that began to run down her face.

"Forgive me, your highness," she replied.

"How is this possible? We have only one piano and two ladies. This will not do. Ah, Maria my dear lady! You think the Czar; the emperor of all Russia who had fought and won so many battles cannot solve such a simple problem! You shall have a European mahogany clavichord. Now, the two of you can play together!"

Leaving the glorious days of Chornaya Graz in the past, my day dream returned to the present century when I heard, "Hurry, the grounds are closing." The tour guide was pushing me along to exit the estate. "Tomorrow, we will fly to historical Leningrad," she said.

I couldn't wait to continue my Soviet Tour of 1967.

15

Historical Leningrad

Located at the east end of the Gulf of Finland and bordered on both banks by the Neva River, the city of Leningrad captivated me. Many vast aged buildings lined the streets of the city and within its walls each building had its own story and history. The main square, Nevsky Prospect, once housed elaborate palaces, but now was used for government offices. The oldest building, Fortress of Peter and Paul, built in 1703 was used as a political prison during Imperial times. The Cathedral of Saint Peter and Paul, where most of the Czars were buried, was located nearby. I reminded myself the brilliance of the city was due to Italian and French architects that built it for Peter the Great.

I was nearing the completion of my tour in the Soviet Union and was pleased that it would end with this beautiful city. I thought Leningrad was an ugly name and did not fit the character of such an elegant place. The name sounded so cold, so rigid. St. Petersburg, the original name was more suitable. It captured the essence of the city, known as *Venice of the North* with its many canals. I made my way to the entrance of the Cathedral of Saint Peter and Paul. The exterior was beautiful, however once I entered, it felt lifeless and made me shiver as the atmosphere was eerily still. My attention turned to the tombs in the rear of the cathedral. One large tomb in particular captured my interest. A red velvet rope encircled it. It contained the remains of Peter the Great. I cautiously took a few steps forward and leaned over the barrier to get a closer look. I held my breath as I read the inscription:

Peter the Great,
born May 30, 1672, died March 8, 1725

Natalia Petrovna,
born Aug 31, 1719 died March 15, 1725

Peter the Great was buried with his 6-year-old daughter, Natalia, who died shortly after him. I stood in silence, not moving, just staring at the tomb. I found it astonishing that I would be standing at the remains of someone who died over 250 years ago. It was as if history had caught up with me — or was it the other way around? Standing at the remains of Peter the Great, I felt as if I was part of an era long gone. *'What would Peter the Great think if he could see the world today?'* His vision was to westernize and enlighten Russia, to reform the country political and economically. I was eager to learn more of the Czar's world. I was happy the following day a trip to the summer palace of Peter the Great would give me that opportunity. I couldn't wait to experience the wonder of his time, to walk in the footsteps of Peter the Great.

It was a glorious morning at the summer palace of Peter the Great. White clouds glided through the blue skies with their reflections resting momentarily on the many golden statues and sparkling water fountains.

A pavilion stood at the far end of the estate. It was Peter the Great's favorite place when he stayed and entertained on the grounds. The pavilion had been built under the direction of a German architect, Johann Friedrich Braunstein, yet it had a French name *Monplaisir* meaning "my pleasure." The charming brick residence overlooked the Gulf of Finland. Light filled arcades with French doors opened to expose a spectacular view of the waters below. Sunflowers grew alongside the building.

I walked to the side with the magnificent yellow floral. I could feel the abundance of sunflowers dazzling on the iris of my eyes. I leaned down to pick one. Why did I seem to recall sunflowers on an oak table, long ago? Had I been intoxicated by the splendor of the outdoors? I had to get a closer look of the interior of the pavilion. I made my way to peer through one of the many arched windows. I put my hand to my forehead, pressing against the windowpane. Spectacular painted ceilings and architecture were prevalent throughout the rooms. The largest room, a ceremonial hall displayed a vaulted ceiling, painted to symbolize the four basic elements in the form of Greek Gods. I walked over to the side with the view of the sea and put my arms on the ornate railing behind me and learned against it, content to bask in the rays of sunshine. I took a deep breath and the fresh sea air rolling in from the Gulf of Finland invigorated me. I felt renewed and full of vitality. It was another world.

"I wish I could stay here forever."

As I sighed, a sense of *déjà vu* overcame me. The summer palace, with its grounds of golden statues and sparkling waters became alive as if transposed into a time that once was 1721 Monplaisir.

In 1721 the maritime atmosphere of *Monplaisir*, and Princess Maria Kantemir, were the Czar's passion. Each had their own unique beauty and the Czar found pleasure in both. Today, Princess Maria would meet the Czar at Monplaisir.

Maria started to make her way up the rocky slopes towards the white terraces of *Monplaisir*. She turned her head back to look at the gray waters of the Gulf of Finland. *How beautiful is the sea today!* thought Maria.

At that moment, a cool spray of seawater from the crashing waves upon the shoreline below caught her face. She did not mind, as it felt refreshing. She loved the feel of the moisture on her face and she would allow it to dissipate on its own. She noticed a large gray rock encircled by wildflowers in the distance above and ran towards it.

I shall sit among the tranquility of the flowers and admire the turmoil of the sea, she decided as she ran to the rock, her hair blowing in the wind. She lifted her fuchsia colored dress and stepped over the yellow and purple flowers that surrounded the rock. She carefully lowered herself to sit on the rock, one arm outstretched in case she missed her footing. She looked at the waters below as foaming white caps surfaced and then disappeared. She shifted her glance upwards, to the seagulls flying above the water, making hungry, squiggly sounds as they searched for their prey of fish.

The wings of the seagulls above the sea, reflecting off the rippling waves, how calm and serene they are, thought Maria.

Mesmerized by the beauty below, she closed her eyes, inhaled the sea air and began to meditate. Hours passed or were it minutes? It did not matter as she was a headstrong woman and Peter understood her ways. As the flowers growing among the turmoil of the rough sea, she was the tranquility in the havoc of his life. She would keep him waiting a bit longer because he would miss her all the more. She opened her eyes and pulled herself up from the rock. It was time to go. She would continue her way up the slope and into the strong arms of her Czar. She followed the path of flowerbeds that weaved in and out among the sparkling fountains that crowned the splendor grounds of *Monplaisir*.

She continued her walk to the pavilion and into the Ceremonial Hall. She looked up at the high vaulted ceilings painted with Greek gods and they seemed to return her gaze. Their eyes followed her as she made her way past the huge canvases depicting nautical scenes that hung from beneath the ceilings. Maria smiled as she walked passed, recalling the Czar's favorite past time of nautical studies. She continued through the oak paneled rooms until she reached the Lacquered Gallery. She opened the double doors to expose a room, so breath taking, that even though she had seen it many times before, she still had to stop and admire the Chinese art, which covered the room. It was decorated in black, red and gold gilt panels of lacquered pavilions, bridges and golden dragons. Next to them, ornamental brackets displayed Chinese porcelains as tall as the exquisite room. The panels and porcelains were further off set in spectacular red lacquer and gold gilt.

Maria closed the doors behind her as she entered. She glanced at the Czar's collection of Dutch and Flemish paintings with their attached crimson ribbons, hanging on the oak paneled walls. Several blue vases of freshly picked yellow sunflowers stood on a long oversized oak table in the center of the room. Peter discovered the ancient floral on a trip to Holland. He liked them so much that he brought the seeds back to Russia and had them planted on the grounds of *Monplaisir*. During Lent, the oil from the sunflower seeds was used during church services.

Maria continued walking until she saw the door to Peter's

bedchamber ahead. She quietly opened it and peered in. The monarch was sitting at the edge of his pastel green, gold trimmed canopy bed that matched the ornate painting on the ceiling. At first, he did not hear her or see her, but the scent of her perfume began to permeate the room and he knew she was there. He rose slowly to greet her. He was at a loss for words. Maria walked towards him. She remained silent. Their eyes met as she neared him. Instinctively, they embraced one another. Words were not needed. They held each other tightly, not daring to move, allowing the warmth of their bodies to penetrate. Lingering in an endless embrace of love, etching the moment in their minds, they dare not let go, falling onto the bed to physically and passionately devour one another. Only after passion drained from their bodies, did their senses return to normal.

"Maria, Maria, how did I function so long without you!" panted Peter. "I have not been living. I have only gone through the motions. You are my life, my breath!"

"My dearest, Peter, I have missed you ever so much. I dream of you when we were apart and when I do, I know you are thinking of me too," Maria whispered ever so softly. Peter did not answer, as he pulled Maria closer to him. He smelled the freshness of her hair and he knew no further words were necessary to express his feeling of contentment as he drifted off to sleep.

Wrapped in his arms, Maria could only think of the pleasures of the day and soon fell asleep in the bliss of *Monplaisir.*

16

Astrakhan, 1722 —
The Persian Campaign

Another war was flaring up on the eastern border of Russia. The country of Persia was in riot and slipping into
anarchy. The internal turmoil would make it an easy target and
a conquest for the Ottoman Turks.

Local tribes had already destroyed the shops and ware-
houses of Russian merchants in Persia. Peter the Great needed
to act fast and get to Persia before the Ottomans. He planned
a military expedition and would leave St. Petersburg at once
to join his armies on the front. He would take his Imperial
Chancellor, Prince Dmitri along who would have administra-
tive command during this mission. The entire Kantemir family set out with Prince Dmitri, to join the Czar. Only Princess
Trubetskaya stayed behind with their infant daughter, Ekaterina *(Smaragda II)*. The infant was just one and a half years old

and was named after Dmitri's older daughter, Smaragda who a few years earlier had died, unable to recover from a bout with the flu.

It was June and the weather was hot and humid. The entire party traveled down the Volga River to the city of Astrakhan on barges; however the cool waters of the Volga gave them little relief from the stifling heat and small tents were put up on the barges to keep the sun at bay. It was a blistering day on the expedition. Antioch stayed put beneath the tents, occasionally peering out to take notes of what he saw of the way of life on the Volga River. What he observed intrigued him, for his prospective of people and serfs along the waterway gave him a clearer idea of the hypocrisies of life. He would write and expose those unjust inequalities in his satires. After a few hours, Antioch sitting in the barge alongside his father put down his quill.

"Father, the life along the Volga is familiar, but yet so foreign," he said.

"Yes Antioch. It is a different life than what you are accustomed to," replied Dmitri.

Dmitri was gathering his own notes into a diary. He too had collected and studied all the traditions of the local people on the way down the Volga River. He would continue to do the same when they reach the Caspian Sea and the town of Derbent. He had just completed reviewing the appeals and manifestos of Peter the Great and translated them into Persian and Tatar. The manifestos were addressed to the people of the Caspian Sea region and to the northern Caucasus province. The papers were to be distributed and read to the populace of the country bringing awareness to the Czar's efforts to better the living conditions of the citizens and for his ideas for a greater Russia.

Antioch and Prince Dmitri were so indulged in their work and studies that they did not pay any attention to the barges that followed one another through the winding channels ahead, and to a woman's laughter coming from the first barge. It was the barge carrying Peter the Great and Princess Maria Kantemir. Maria was pregnant with the Czar's child and had joined the expedition at the Czar's request. Peter was hoping with the pregnancy, a male heir would ensure the future of Russia. His wife Catherine was unable to give him a son as the eight children she had with him all died in infancy, except for two daughters. As a result, she had gotten fat and unattractive. Peter admired Princess Maria for her soft beauty and freshness. She was what he saw as desirable and he lavished all his attentions towards her.

Catherine was in the second barge and she could not bear the laughter or her husband's infidelity for all to witness. She was fully aware of the situation and had ignored it as there was nothing she could do. She would have to be patient as she knew her moment would come. She wondered if she had the courage to do what others have suggested. She would have to wait; wait until the right opportunity presented itself. A chance of distance and separation between Peter and Maria would be all that was needed for what she had in mind. It would then that she would play her hand as it was no different than a game of cards. One just needed the right moves carefully thought through to be the victor. Catherine would pretend to share Peter's hope for a future heir even though she was aware what the birth would mean to her.

Catherine settled comfortably in her barge for she would not let her thoughts get the better of her; instead, she would enjoy the scenery. She waved at the people who had lined the river to send their greetings to the Czar. As she looked ahead, she noticed the sailors in the front barge had rested their oars.

At the stern was her husband Peter. Her barge was getting closer to his. As it got nearer, Peter sprang over the narrow waters and jumped into Catherine's barge. She leaned back in her seat, taken aback by this action. Catherine wondered what he wanted. He was a handsome sight with his sunburned rugged face and she still found him desirable and wondered if he felt the same about her.

Had he left Princess Maria to be with her? Did Princess Maria know Peter had joined her in the barge? She did not get further in her thoughts for Peter sat down beside her.

"Well, your Empress, how are you enjoying this wonderful travel down the Volga?" he asked.

"I love the weather and the people of our country," replied Catherine.

"Tomorrow, we will reach Astrakhan and then on to the Caspian," said Peter.

"All of us?" asked Catherine who had Maria Kantemir on her mind.

"No, the princess is near her time and all the women will stay behind. All the women except you, of course. I cannot fight without you by my side."

"What? The great Peter needs a woman by his side during battle?" laughed Catherine.

Loud roars interrupted her sentence, as villagers had run to the riverbed to greet the Czar. Peter leaped to his feet pulling Catherine up by her arm and drawing her close to his side. They both waved to the crowd as Peter further embraced Catherine in his happy mood. Later into the evening, Catherine learned from one of the servants that Princess Maria and Czar Peter had a quarrel.

Well, my little pretty one. I am not finished with you yet! thought Catherine.

Maria was relieved to stop her journey in Astrakhan as she was tired and not used to such hardships. This was not a life style Maria was accustomed to. In her present condition she could not endure any further travel. Peter too, wanted Maria to get some rest and to spare her any further discomfort. She would wait for him in Astrakhan, while he continued on to battle near the Caspian Sea with Catherine alongside him. It was Catherine's custom to always accompany her husband to combat. Maria knew this and accepted it. She did not like the fact that Peter could not bear to be without Catherine during his times on the battlefield. But never mind, Maria had the upper hand as she knew Peter was in love with her.

When he returned from battle, happy news would await him. She would present him with the male child that he so desired. After all, Peter had left his trusted Greek Doctor Palikala to look after her. There was no need to worry.

Czar Peter's army left Astrakhan with 23,000 soldiers to join ships on the Caspian Sea for Derbent. Later 100,000 more Cossacks, Kalmuks and Tatars were to join them on the land route. After a few minor skirmishes, the Czar made entry into Derbent on August 23, 1722. As he ventured deeper into the region of Derbent he realized his preparations were insufficient just like the battle at Moldavia, eleven years earlier. He could not afford such a disastrous repeat.

Through it all Catherine was keeping up the morale of the soldiers. They were suffering from heat, thirst, and hunger. She joked with the officers, encouraging them to move on and Peter couldn't help but admire her for her courage and good humor. He wanted to continue on to the city of Baku, but it would be another thirty days march and the Russian army was too exhausted. He would instead return to Astrakhan to see how Princess Maria was doing. He informed his generals to remain stationary in his absence and on his return, the campaign would resume when sufficient forces arrived. He was thankful for Catherine who was always by his side, but he was more concerned about Princess Maria. She would be the future of Russia alongside him with their newborn. She was in the hands of Palikala, his most trusted and personal physician. All would be well.

What Peter did not know was that Catherine took this opportunity to bribe the doctor. Little greedy Palikala could not resist the temptation of precious stones, coins and if he succeeded, a house in the country with a multitude of serfs. Catherine had given him an offer he could not and would not refuse. He was one of the best and most faithful doctors in the royal household. No one would suspect anything as his medical expertise would guide him to disguise any improprieties, but would he have the courage to go through with what Catherine had ordered and what he had promised to do?

On Peter's return to Astrakhan, Prince Dmitri was the first to greet the Czar. Peter shivered when he saw the expression on Dmitri's face. There could be nothing but bad news. As Dmitri whispered into Peter's ear, a look of agony distorted his sun burnt face and his body quivered so hard that he had to lean on a nearby tree for support. He did not speak as his twisted face told all.

The Czar hung his head to his shoulders and walked away. Prince Dmitri need say no more as it was evident what had happened. Even Catherine became concerned. This was not her plan, at least not for Peter. She did not want him to get any sicker than he was. Lately, he suffered from stomach problems and this news caused him to double over with unbearable pain. The intolerable heat, his indigestion and now bad news greeted him on his return from the battlefront. He looked ghastly.

Catherine felt sorry, but it did not stop her from secretly enjoying her bittersweet moment. She could not help but look the other way in triumph, trying to conceal her smile. She knew her plan had succeeded. It was obvious. Maria's child had been stillborn. Contentment is what she felt when she saw Doctor Palikala rushing to Peter to express his sorrow for the loss.

"It's nature; it's not meant to be. A baby boy, born dead," he muttered.

"Stop, I will hear no more. I wish to be left alone. Look to your daughter," Czar Peter said sternly to Prince Dmitri.

He walked away and out of sight with his head hanging down even further; least anyone see the tears of sorrow in the eyes of Peter the Great. Even in his moment of grief, he was still the Czar of all Russia. He would not let his anguish be shown.

Catherine stood speechless. She could not believe her plan had succeeded. The Greek doctor had the courage to do what was expected of him. She leaned against a railing for support. God willing no one would learn, or hopefully, suspect her of any involvement. She would deny it of course, as there was no proof. Catherine pretended to sympathize with the Czar over the misfortune, however secretly she was relieved for she had triumphed.

In the course of the days, there were all kinds of rumors and they reached Peter's ears. Peter did not believe it; Catherine would not dare to play a hand in his misfortune. She would not be so foolish, but then he knew she was strong willed and did what she wanted. Yes, he should suspect that she was behind it, however not directly. Most likely, Catherine's loyal maidservants had given Maria some kind of poison to cause the misfortune. That could be the only explanation.

Peter had to get on with the affairs of the state and duties as *father and protector of Russia.* He was furious, but there was nothing he could do. He did not feel well. Perhaps, it was all too much for him, the battle and the loss of a successor. He would hurry north, to the waters of a newly discovered mineral spring. His kidneys were acting up and his doctors said it would be best for him to go there for treatment. Heeding his doctor's advice and in unrelenting pain, Peter left abruptly with no further thoughts of Catherine and Maria who now had to fend for themselves.

Princess Maria, weak from pain, both physically and mentally, proceeded to Dmitrievskoe, a Kantemir estate in the south of Russia to recuperate.

Catherine decided to return to St. Petersburg and wait for Peter there.

When Peter reached the northern portion of Russian feeling somewhat better, he decided to ignore his doctor's advice for treatment at the springs and continued on to St. Petersburg. He had received word that his armies had taken Baku and proclaimed a Russian victory. The good news overshadowed his anger of the unexpected events in Astrakhan. A celebration of conquest was in order. Though, the Czar did not feel completely well, he would not deprive his people and country of a victory celebration. They should be reminded of the accomplishments of a great Russia and its ruler.

A costume party with fireworks was arranged. Peter dressed as a Catholic cardinal read the official documents of his victory of not only Baku, but of Persia too. He would proclaim a Russian triumph to all the guests and have a party that would last for days. Shouts of joy greeted the opening day of the festivities. Catherine appeared on the balcony of the palace dressed in the costume of a great Venetian lady. Czar Peter stepped out after her and the crowd roared. Catherine turned towards Peter and began with her public salutation;

"Russia's great ruler, Russia's great savior, I toast you my husband on your victory."

She handed him a drink to celebrate the glory and Czar Peter proceeded to take one big gulp from the glass. He enjoyed the merriment of the occasion and waved to the crowd as they waved back with shouts of praise for the great Czar of Russia. He took Catherine's arm and they returned inside the palace to make their way to the grand ballroom. The first guest Czar Peter noticed was Prince Dmitri Kantemir. He was dressed as a Sultan with a big turban encrusted with pearls and diamonds on his head. His children followed behind in Turkish dress. Peter's eyes glanced about as he was hoping to see Princess Maria, but she was not with her family. It was too soon after the tragedy to think she would join them. She had lost their infant son and almost her life as well. He was too selfish to think that she might be here to share in the victory celebration of his latest battle.

"Boom! Boom! Boom!"

Spectacular fireworks with dazzling colors of red, yellow and orange lit the skies. The entire estate was aglow in lights.

Vases containing an array of flowers covered every table. They were in the foyers, on the statues and overflowed onto the grounds.

Midgets entertained the crowd with their tricks. Musicians strolled about playing harmonious tunes. Costumed ladies and gentlemen excitedly joined hands to form a circle. They took turns to push each other into the center. The one with the grandest and most unique costume received applause and howls of approval from the crowd. Feathers and opera masks dominated the celebration.

It was impossible to choose the best costumed individual.

Such was the gaiety of the celebration that by ten o'clock at night, there were one thousand empty bottles strewed about the estate.

Even, the servants were drunk, but then, no one noticed.

17

A Death and a Final Wish

Princess Maria returned to Dmitrievskoe, her father's estate near Slobidska, Ukraine. The doctors had ordered her to take extended rest for she was extremely ill and needed time to recuperate from the loss of her infant. She barely survived the trip and when she arrived at the estate she was delirious with fever and in and out of consciousness. She envisioned Czar Peter holding their newborn with his arm around her, beaming with pride. It was when her eyes opened that reality set in. She wished she could sleep forever for she found life was unbearable now.

The touch of a cool washcloth on her forehead woke her and she opened her eyes and looked down at the light blanket that covered her. She turned her head to the side to see a nurse standing at a nearby table, pouring water, from a pitcher into a glass. She struggled to say something, but only illegible words came from her mouth. The unexpected rambling of words startled the nurse who quickly set her glass down and ran to Maria.

"Princess, you will get better. Do not try to talk, just rest."

Maria closed her eyes as she did not want to wake up. She wanted to go back to Astrakhan and change the hands of fate. She wanted Czar Peter and she wanted to hold their infant boy. Her heart ached for them both. A bolt of pain shot through Maria's body and she screamed out for the Czar.

"Peter, Peter!"

The nurse hurriedly gave her a glass of water diluted with a soothing potion to drink. Maria's body trembled and her head fell back on the pillow. The potion dulled the pain and within a few moments Maria drifted into an endless sleep.

A slight breeze swept across Maria's cheek. The light airy wind blowing through the open window caused the long white lace curtains to rustle against the wall. Maria breathed in the morning air. She turned over and opened her eyes to see the sun rising over the horizon. How long has she slept, how long has she been here? She lifted her head from the pillow. Then, she remembered! Her head fell back on the pillow and she began to weep. Her sobbing bought in Antioch who heard her cries. He had been busy writing in the adjacent room.

"Maria, Maria, you are well. We were all so worried your fever would not break. You need more rest and we will take care of you. You will get better here. You will be afar from the busy life of the royal courts. You will have tranquility and quiet and I shall sit by your side and read my new satires. Are you up for some tea?" asked Antioch.

Maria nodded her head.

"Where are the servants when you need them?" asked Antioch, anxiously poking his head out into the hallway. One of the servants saw Antioch and hastily approached him.

"Natasha, there you are. Thank goodness! Maria's fever has

broken. Please, we need some tea and don't forget the honey. It will do her good now that she's recovering," he said.

"Yes sir, right away sir," replied Natasha as she rushed off whispering to all the servants, "Maria's awake. Maria's awake," as she passed along her way to the kitchen.

Prince Dmitri heard the commotion and Natasha's muttering as she whizzed past the study where he was writing. He would take this time to fulfill an unspoken promise; a promise made to his late wife Cassandra on her deathbed. He would act immediately. He had not been feeling well since his return from the Persian campaign. He walked towards the library of books that lined the walls of the room. There was a section in particular that he was looking for, the section that contained his writings on the *History of the Growth and Decay of the Ottoman Empire*. His fingers moved across the many books until they stopped at the three volumes of black covered, gold trimmed manuscripts. He carefully moved them aside exposing a small area of a bare wall that had a dusty gold clasp attached to it.

Prince Dmitri lifted the clasp which opened to further reveal a deep hole in the wall. He reached in and pulled out a purple velvet bag. It had not been opened since it was first sealed. It contained precious jewels and mementos. He had not touched it since his wife Cassandra's death. It was her desire to have her valuables given to her daughter Maria. Dmitri would fulfill her wish, as was his wish. These jewels would be passed down through the centuries to Boris Kantemir.

He knew he did not have much time left as he had been in occasional pain and had a dizziness that at times overtook him. He accompanied Peter the Great from the Dneiper River to the Caucasus Mountains, from the Caspian Sea, and to the banks of the Moscow River during the Persian campaign. The expedition along with Maria's misfortune of losing the newborn took a toll on his health. Now his sakharry bolezn (sugar disease) was acting up. Never mind, he would cope with it as he had before. He would not let the disease overtake his life for he still had unfinished affairs to attend to. Only Dmitri knew of the existence of the purple velvet bag that lay behind the hidden wall. He hesitated, he dared not open it for fear it would unleash the past and he was not prepared to grieve once again for his beloved Cassandra.

All that was, is all that passed and so it will be with me and with all of us when our time comes. *I need to tend to my daughter for she has suffered greatly,* thought Dmitri.

He proceeded out of the study to the grand hallway and to the far end of the palace. He was having difficulty walking and barely reached Maria's room without collapsing. He did not remember the velvet bag being so heavy. He leaned against the wall to catch his breath before opening the door to Maria's bedchamber. He did not want her to know he was feeling so ill. After a moment's rest, he recovered and opened the door to her room. Without saying a word he walked over and gave her a kiss on her forehead.

Maria needed no words to understand what her father felt. She looked up at him and he looked very tired and for the first time he looked old. Only his regal demeanor remained unchanged. Maria glanced down at the purple velvet bag he was holding. She had seen it often on her mother's dressing table. The velvet bag contained her mother's most treasured possessions. Her mother would pour the contents out when deciding which piece of jewelry was most fitting to wear for formal affairs. There was only one reason her father was hold-ing the precious bag. Maria knew it belonged to her now. It was her inheritance from her mother who inherited it from her mother and she from her mother. The valuable Byzantine jewels were passed from one Cantacuzene to another. The centuries old prized jewels could not replace her mother, but wearing them Maria knew she would feel closer to her mother and to her Greek ancestors who sat on the throne of the Eastern Empire.

Dmitri handed the bag to Maria. He was too tired to speak and remained silent as she took the bag. Maria put the bag on her lap and untied the silver ribbons that held it together.

"Papa, it's beautiful!" she exclaimed as she pulled a sparkling silver ewer and basin from a sack that was in the larger velvet bag.

Dmitri's eyes began to swell as he stared at the basin set and recalled the time, so long ago in the court of the Sultan when an atmosphere of anticipation and happiness surrounded the ewer and basin.

"That was a gift from your grandfather, Serban Cantacuzene on the occasion of your mother's marriage to me. I have only fond memories of this ewer and basin. It belongs to you now. May it bring you the happiness that I found with your mother," he hoarsely whispered.

He was finding it difficult to speak and tried to limit his words, but could not contain himself as he recalled Cassandra pouring water from the ewer at the Sultan's palace in Istanbul.

"My darling daughter, in addition, I have my own personal gift of ten thousand rubles. It will not replace the lost of your son, who would have been the future heir of Russia, but it will give you the security needed in later life after I am gone."

Maria began to sob. She had her chance of an imperialistic future and along with it almost lost her life. What would she do now? Her future was uncertain. She knew her brothers leaned on her for advice and for her good wisdom. She was the strong, sensible one and always managed to resolve problems fairly. She did not use emotion to deal with issues as did her brothers. She hoped they would continue to depend on her as they always had in the past.

A sudden surge of energy caused Maria to lean up from her bed and glance out the window. In the far off distance she could see the many serfs on the grounds of her family's estate. They were like little ants scurrying about and attending to the fields, as if ants in a colony. Maria felt sorry for them. The Kantemir family had thousands of serfs and she knew they were suffering, as this summer there was a drought. They would have to work extra hard on the land to produce crops.

Even in her worse time, Maria was caring and compassionate. She had to deal with her misery, just as the serfs had to deal with the drought. She understood and sympathized with them. It was not easy to overcome any crises. Was she much different than the serfs? Yes, they were in fact, very much similar. The only difference was that she was born into privilege. Did that mean the nobility were better and immune from the misfortunes of life? What does one do with the circumstance in which one finds them? Does one stay still, do nothing and give up just existing going through the motions of life? Or does one have the strength of will to put meaning in themselves and others and carry on? In the end all have to answer to the same maker.

Maria pondered this thought for a while. She would ask Antioch his belief. She had a high regard for his opinions for they were profound and logical.

Months passed. Princess Maria continued to recuperate at her father's estate, but as her health improved Dmitri's declined. His sugar diabetes had gotten out of control and was taking over his body. Every day he was getting weaker as he could no longer walk and was in constant pain. The pain caused him much irritability and fatigue for numbness had set in both his hands and feet. His vision became blurred and he could no longer see clearly. He needed constant help and was confined to a bed as he was unable to move about.

Maria's health returned and with help from the servants, she cared continually for Dmitri. The doctors said it was hopeless and only a matter of time. Prince Dmitri knew this and prepared his will. He instructed his children to concern themselves with their education. He further stipulated that whoever, excelled the most in their studies would be the heir of his estates. He stated that Antioch, the youngest was the most intelligent and best for learning.

As Dmitri lay unconscious, he did not realize that the indecisiveness in his will would eventually lead to lengthy family disputes. Each day the children visited their father in his bedchamber. They looked at his lifeless body hoping that he would improve as he had in the past, but it did not happen.

Dmitri passed away August 21, 1723, two months short of his 50th birthday. The very day he died, he was awarded the title of Reichsfurst *(Prince) of the Holy Roman Empire* by Charles VI.

On October 1, 1723, Prince Dmitri's widow, Princess Anastasia Trubetskaya and his children delivered the black draped coffin to Moscow's *Constantine and Elena Church* at the Greek Nikolsky Monastery. There, in accordance with Dmitri's wishes, in a modest gathering he was laid to rest beside his first wife, Cassandra Cantacuzene who had been re-interred there from her original resting place on the small island at Chornaya Graz, and their daughter Smaragda. (Prince Dmitri Kantemir's remains eventually would be transferred by the Soviet Union in 1930 to Iasi, Romania where he rests in the *Church of the Three Hierach's*.)

With her father gone, Princess Maria at 23 years of age would take on the role as a valuable mentor to her four brothers, Constantine, Matvei, Sergei and Antioch.

18

Revenge

Peter was not happy with his wife, Catherine. He suspected she might have taken a lover, a handsome chamberlain named William Mons, a German born in Russia. Mons was Catherine's secretary and confidant. Peter could not confirm it, even though he found them one evening in the gardens in a compromising position. He assumed there was a romantic liaison between the two. To make matters worse, he heard rumors that Mons was taking bribes from Catherine's estate. The situation would have to be handled diplomatically and with care. He would not display any signs of anger. He would continue his normal activities with Catherine, even though they hardly spoke. He did not want his intentions to be known.

Peter walked through the main palace he shared with Catherine to the dining room. The servants noticing a look of discontent on the Czar's face hastily opened the double doors to allow him entry into the formal room. Peter was to dine with

Catherine, their daughters Anna and Elizabeth and William Mons. He entered and noticed Catherine seated at the end of the long rectangular dining table. Anna and Elizabeth sat alongside each other and Mons was seated directly across from the two princesses. Peter took his seat at the opposite end of the table from Catherine, scrutinizing her and Mons as he sat down. He was very displeased this evening putting him in a foul mood and not even the aroma of a tantalizing roast duck, potatoes and cabbage that lay on the table could entice him. He picked at the meat moving it about his plate. When he could no longer contain himself he blurted out.

"I am tired. I think we should all retire."

Everyone looked up at him. They had not finished eating and were surprised at his outburst. Catherine looked at the watch that was fastened to her gown.

"It is only 9:00p.m," she answered.

Peter discerned himself from Catherine's words. He wanted to be rid of her and Mons.

"You are mistaken!" he shouted as he grabbed the watch off her dress. He opened the case of the watch and swiveled the time ahead to read twelve o' clock.

"It is midnight and everyone will go to bed!"

He flung the watch back into Catherine's lap. No one dared to say a word. The Czar's family rose from their places at the table, quietly and nervously retiring to their rooms. William Mons had no choice, but to get up and leave as well. He would return home to finish his dinner as he knew better than to further infuriate the Czar when he was in a rage.

Once home and having eaten, Mons was enjoying his after dinner drink and a fine cigar when the doors burst open and before he could comprehend what was happening, he was surrounded by soldiers.

"You are under arrest!" they shouted as they pushed him

out of his home and into a wagon that took him to the Peter and Paul Fortress.

There, he was thrown into a dark musty cell. The only opening was a door with bars across a small window that allowed the guards to watch his every movement. Mons scratched his head as he lay on the stone floor. He wondered if Czar Peter knew about the relationship between him and the Czar's wife. He would deny everything and of course he would not admit any relationship with Catherine.

The next morning Mons was questioned about the bribes he had taken against Catherine's estate. This caught him off guard, as he was not prepared to handle accusation of corruption. He had expected to be questioned on his supposed affair with the Czar's wife and not the bribery. He had no answer and therefore had no choice, but to admit guilt. The soldiers wasted no time in preparing their weapons of torture. When Mons saw this, he felt faint and slumped against the legs of one of the soldiers, but it was only a temporary escape from what was to come. They threw brandy in his face and pulled him to his feet. He was revived for a short time until he saw the Czar enter the cell. His eyelids fluttered and he fainted again.

"No, he is not a true Russian. We will not torture him," said Peter.

Slowly, Mons regained consciousness and he confessed to all the accusations of bribery against him. He confessed to taking money from Catherine's estate. Nothing was mentioned of any affair with Catherine nor did the Czar ask any questions of any improprieties between them. The Czar did not show any curiosity nor would he acknowledge any unfaithfulness between his wife and Mons. The admission of taking bribes was enough for punishment and retaliation. The interrogation was completed. A declaration of death would be carried out. There would be no reprisal! Mons was frozen with fear, but he was confident that Catherine would protect him from the consequences. He was waiting for her to intercede, but she was nowhere in sight. He strained his neck looking through the window of his cell trying to see if she was approaching, but all was quiet in the darken hallway. Where was Catherine? His body shivered with convulsions with the realization that he was on his own and Catherine would not save him from his demise.

Catherine displayed no reaction when she learned of the sentencing. She carried on normally, even taking minuet dance lessons with her daughters on the day of the execution. She would not give Peter the satisfaction of her true feelings. Her servants told her how brave and handsome Mons looked in his fur coat as he walked to the scaffolds. He acknowledged his friends along the way and bowing to them. He climbed the stairs to the executioner's rope showing none of the cowardly behavior he had displayed earlier when interrogated by Czar Peter.

Standing tall, he took off his fur coat; loose strands of fine brown hair blew around his face in the cold stormy November air. He could have not looked more distinguished in his white tail shirt and dark trousers. A black hood was put over his head and in a matter of seconds his body swung from the scaffold. All was silent and eerie. Peter could not help, but admire Mon's courage, but he was not yet finished. Catherine would need to learn a lesson as well. He would take her for a sleigh ride the next morning. He would not let her forget so easily.

"Come Catherine, the fresh air would do us both some good after a day full of gloom. We should enjoy this sunny day," said Peter.

They got into the open sleigh and covered themselves with a fur blanket to keep warm. Three horses with chiming red and gold bells attached to their necks pulled the sleigh through the crisp white snow. Catherine enjoyed the beauty of the frost covered country with icicles hanging from every tree branch. She was feeling content with the surrounding beauty when the sleigh slowed down. It passed the scaffold where Mon's body still lay on the frozen ground. As they passed Peter gripped her hand and forced her to take a further look. Catherine's face showed no emotion. She was aware of the consequences of betrayal and of Peter's rage. She had no intention to join Mons in his demise.

"How sad, there should be such corruption, even in a royal court," she said.

Her acknowledgment pacified Peter and diminished any further thoughts of fury. "Horseman, take us back to the palace," he shouted.

After the execution of Mons, Czar Peter's and Catherine's relationship began to deteriorate further. He spent most of his time with Princess Maria. He spoke with Catherine only when it was necessary, however, tonight was an exception for Peter and Catherine would dine together. During dinner, not a word was said between the two and their mood matched the stillness of the dimly lit room.

"It is I who am tired now. Please allow me to retire to my bed chamber," said Catherine.

Peter nodded his head, for he had a purpose in asking Catherine to join him for dinner this evening. A surprise would be waiting for her.

Catherine entered her bedchamber. She sat down at her dressing table and noticed a large jar which had not been there before. She leaned forward for a closer look. She gasped and put her hand over mouth, lest her screams should be heard. She was repulsed at the sight, for sealed in alcohol spirits, Mons head was glaring at her.

Standing behind the half opened bedchamber door to Catherine's room, Peter smiled. He was satisfied that he had his revenge. Catherine was his wife and he would not harm her, but she had to know that Peter was the Czar and he ruled with strength and if necessary with terror. He knew how to deal with her and hers. He returned to his study and closed the door behind him walking straight to the desk opposite the lit fireplace. He took a key from his pocket and unlocked one of the drawers. Reaching into the drawer he took out a gold cloth that held a rolled white scroll. With a grin, he threw the gold cloth on the floor. He did not bother to look at the scroll for he knew its contents. Tearing the document into pieces he angrily threw it into the fireplace.

"So, Catherine assumes she will rule after me. I will not allow it. Dosvedaneya, my last will and testament, Catherine will not be the future of Russia. It will be one who has my eternal love. I shall prepare a new document."

He sat at his desk and poured a shot of brandy into a glass. He gulped it down rapidly as he sat for a few moments deliberating the events of the last few days.

"To you Mons," he toasted the dead man, pouring another short of brandy, only to gulp it down faster.

"One toast deserves another. May you rest in peace, Mons."

He refilled his glass once more. By now the Czar was drunk and all his thoughts forgotten, except for Princess Maria. He missed her and needed her. He would summon for her.

'No one can ever replace or be compared to my beloved sweet Maria,' he thought as he staggered up from his chair to ring for the courier.

"Your highness?" questioned the courier as he entered Peter's study.

Taking a quill in hand, Peter scribbled some words on ivory paper. He placed the paper into a matching ribbed envelope that was embedded with the gold seal of a double-headed eagle.

"Take this immediately to the Princess Kantemir," he said.

Overcome by drunkenness, he stumbled to the floor and lay there until the Princess arrived.

"Peter, Peter, you have done it now! Let me help you to the bed," said Maria trying to move him.

Peter could not budge and Maria could not move his large frame. All she could do was to hold his head as he vomited into a nearby bucket. When he could vomit no more, she held a cool cloth to his forehead and lay on the floor beside him and soon fell asleep.

Sensing Maria beside him, the Czar smiled and wrapped his arms around her, joining her in sleep, forgetting about the document he was to prepare specifying a new successor.

19

Halic (Changes)

Peter's health, caused by years of drinking began to weaken. His tremors occurred more frequently; even his ivory-eagle headed cane could not help him walk any longer. He did not realize the seriousness of his condition and ignored the reoccurring pain. He continued to attend to the affairs of governing Russia. His latest venture was to travel by boat to visit an iron works factory near the Gulf of Finland.

After completion of the mission and on his return to St. Petersburg in his yacht, he noticed a boat in the distance that was completely out of control. The waves and winds were pushing it, pounding the boat and threatening to capsize it. The vessel was full with soldiers that could not swim. They were paralyzed with the fear of drowning and were shouting for help. Listening to their cries, the Czar could no longer contain himself. He jumped into the sea, swimming to save the men in the stranded boat.

The sight of the Czar swimming in the waters startled the men; however after regaining their senses they followed his instructions. Lines were thrown from other boats and with the Czar's help the marooned boat with its occupants was pulled to the safety of the shore. Dripping wet and grateful that they were saved, the soldiers flocked the Czar, patting him on the back and expressing devotion to their great hero. Peter was pleased with himself for not one man was lost. He had saved the entire crew and could now return to his yacht to rid himself of wet clothing. Throwing his wet clothes on the floor and changing into dry ones, he sat down to pour himself a shot of vodka. A stiff drink is exactly what he needed to warm himself from the cold of the chilly waters. He climbed into bed, covered himself with a thick down-feathered blanket and drifted off to sleep.

During the night he developed a fever accompanied by chills and his body ached and he had a terrible headache. The symptoms came on suddenly and were so alarming that his yacht briskly sailed back to St. Petersburg for medical help. There, the doctors were able to cure him after a week's rest, but his health continued to be fragile thereafter.

By mid-January of 1725 the coolness between Peter and Catherine seemed to diminish; Peter did not have the strength to argue. He had developed a serious infection of the bladder and intestine. The disease was too advanced for any treatment. The doctors ordered bed rest and hoped for the best however, the infection continued to worsen causing Peter to suffer a serious relapse.

Princess Maria, having heard of Peter's dire condition, had managed to gain entry into his bedchambers. She was not prepared to see him in such a state. He was oblivious to everything and everyone. He did not hear or see anything in his unconsciousness state. He was pale and unresponsive. Maria knew the situation was hopeless and she was devastated. She had lost her father a year earlier and now she would lose her love, the Czar of all Russia. She took a white lace handkerchief to dab the tears from her eyes. She made the sign of a cross with her hand and leaned forward to give Peter a kiss on his cheek.

As she did, his eyes opened. They were distant and then they fluttered closed. For a moment, Maria thought he had recognized her. She put her tear stained handkerchief into his hand, squeezing it very hard, whispering into his ear, "My memories of love will always be memories of you. My love will die with you, for I shall never love again."

She felt a weak squeeze in return.

Several members of the assembly in the room were weeping. It was time to leave, no more words, no more touches. Nothing could be done. She was going to be strong, as Peter would have wanted. With farewells set aside, Maria walked out of the room. Catherine would be coming in soon and she did not want any confrontation.

She turned to take one last look as she exited the Czar's room. He was crying out from pain and was calling for his eldest daughter, Anna Petrovna. Maria saw Catherine enter the bedchamber from another door, ever so swiftly. *Catherine is up to something, even in the Czar's final hours*, thought Maria as she walked down the darken hallway, out of the palace grounds and into the drizzle of the morning skies. She walked faster now, her long skirt flowing in the breeze. Her eyes swelled with tears as she realized the happiest time of her life would die with the Czar.

Catherine knelt down besides Peter's bed. Unknown, to all, she had taken a sip of brandy to get her through this ordeal. The small brandy bottle was still clutched in her hand as she threw herself on Peter, crying and praying that he may be released from the torment of death. She lay down besides the Czar and took a swallow once more from the bottle before she laid her head next to his, dozing into a brief sleep. Long groans and the jerking of Peter's head awoke her. Catherine recognized the signs of death and screamed. She could not control herself any longer and began weeping.

Orthodox priests ran into the room and quickly began to pray for the soul of Peter.

"Anna, I want Anna. I want my daughter," groaned Peter.

"Papa, I am here," answered Anna who had just darted into the room.

"My will, I want to give all to . . ."

The white lace handkerchief fell from the Czar's hand. His last breath rattled in his throat and he could not finish what he had to say. Only the half-finished bottle of brandy lay between Peter and Catherine. She still had the mind to pick it up and hide it out of sight, for she did not wish others to see it. She slid the brandy bottle under her sleeve; looking ever so sheepish she slipped to the floor with a great cry.

"O Lord, I pray Thee, open thy paradise to receive unto thyself this great soul."

Bong! Bong! Bong! The echoing notes of the funeral bell sounded and as if on cue, Catherine pulled out the brandy from her sleeve and finished the last drop.

It was February 8, 1725, six o'clock in the morning. The soul of Russia was gone.

PETER THE GREAT: March 8, 1725—Feofan Prokopovich's Funeral Sermon. "What is this and what have we lived to see, O Russians? What are we doing now? We are burying Peter the Great! Is it not a dream? Not a vision of the night? Oh, what a real sorrow! Oh, what certain bitter reality! Contrary to all expectations his life has come to an end much too soon.

The glorious one has been the cause of our innumerable benefactions and joys, who has resuscitated Russia as if from the dead, and has raised it to great power and glory, nay, has begot it and brought it up. He was the true father of his country, whom for his and all the good sons of Russia wished to be immortal, and whom, on account of his youth and bodily strength, they had hoped to see many years alive now gone. O dire calamity, alas his life has ended just as he was beginning to live—behind him was his labors, the unrest, many sorrows and yet victories."

The many government officials, military regiments and foreign dignitaries who crowded the cathedral of *Peter and Paul* in St. Petersburg on a cold snowy day, heard the words of Feofan Prokopovich, but could not fathom the realization of what they were witnessing. They came to pay their respects and see for themselves. Could the father of Russia be truly gone?

Maria leaned against Antioch. She could barely stand as she felt faint. She could no longer listen to or even accept the fact that Peter was gone. The majestic sermon words of Feofan Prokopovich echoing throughout the cathedral could not consul her and only made her feel worse. No one understood that the greatest love of her life was gone.

She was weak, did not feel well and was finding it difficult to breathe. An indescribable emotion overtook Maria and she swooned towards Antioch. She had to get out of the cathedral, away from the huddled dark and gloomy faces of the crowd, all seemingly peering at her. She lowered her head, grateful that she had worn a black lace veil to cover her tormented face. Antioch, seeing Maria was not feeling well, took her by the arm. She leaned on him as he escorted her out of the cathedral of Peter and Paul. Several people glanced towards their direction as they made their way to the exit. Some could be heard whispering as they pushed against each other to get a better view.

"That is Princess Maria Kantemir. It is rumored the Czar left all to her on his deathbed, including the throne," one mourner was heard to say.

"That is only a rumor. It is said he left all to his daughter Anna Petrovna."

"It is also said that on his deathbed, the great Czar said, give all to, but could not finish the sentence. Give all to whom? Alas, we shall never have the answer to that great mystery," replied another.

"Well, it is either Princess Maria or his daughter, Princess Anna," added a dignitary as he observed Princess Anna, standing at the side of the coffin that contained her father's body.

Princess Anna dressed in a black mourning gown, wore a matching black veiled hat that partially hid her face. She stood tall, and expressionless next to the casket, amid an ocean of white lilies that surrounded her and the casket.

"Princess Anna is beautiful, has a great wit and greatly resembles her father and she is highly educated and speaks several languages, Italian, French, German and Swedish. Princess Anne is goodhearted and surely, her father had her in mind as his successor, but since there is no will, Catherine will be the benefactor of all," continued the dignitary with his statement.

Princess Maria managed to stagger out the door where she vomited on the snow-covered grounds of the Peter and Paul cathedral.

"O men of Russia, what do we see? What do we do? This is Peter the Great whom we are committing to the earth," echoed the voice of Prokopovich as Antioch closed the cathedral door behind him. Maria put her hands to her ears. She wanted to hear no more.

"Bring the carriage around. We are leaving, the lady is not well," Antioch said to the horseman.

Maria was seriously ill, however, her physicians could not find any physical disorder. It was said that she was dying of a broken heart and had lost the will to live. Thus there was no antidote for her ailment and she was told to put her affairs in order. She lay in bed in her father's palace overlooking the frozen Neva River where Antioch had taken her after the funeral service for Peter. It had become Antioch's home after their father's death and now it had become her solace too. In her dismal state, Maria prepared her will. She did not want to leave her estate in indecisiveness as her father had done, creating unnecessary turmoil within the family.

She took the quill to hand and began to write, "I leave all my personal belongings and properties to my dear brother Antioch Kantemir who has provided me with love and emotional support in my darkest hours. I do not expect to survive this ailment, which has no name. It does not matter, for nothing remains for me. Antioch has an entire future with his gift of wisdom and writing. What I have belongs to him. May he follow our father's wishes and teachings for he possesses the wisdom of our ancestors. — With humble respects, Princess Maria Kantemir."

20

High Hopes and Expectations

Things however, did not turn out as expected. For some curious reason, some phenomenon, or perhaps it was not to be, Maria's health suddenly improved. She had spent the entire time in St. Petersburg recuperating after the Czar's death.

During her recovery period, Catherine I, Peter's wife had assumed power and the throne. She was popular with the members of the supreme council and she favored the aristocrats who in turn supported her in their efforts to promote their own positions. The council was made up of common men, who had been promoted on the basis of their merits by her husband, Peter the Great. They were anxious to advance their personal interests and proclaimed Catherine as the new Empress of Imperial Russia and the first woman to rule upon her husband's death.

Catherine's and Peter's older daughter, Elizabeth was overlooked as the obvious heir. With Czar Peter gone, and no documents to state otherwise, thoughts of Princess Maria, once considered the Czar's choice as a possible successor quickly faded away. It did not matter for Maria did not want to be a part of her rivalry's Russia. She had no desire to return to society or to the Imperial way of life. Czar Peter with his unique ideas for a better Mother Russia was gone. Life would never be the same. With this in mind, Maria decided to move to Moscow to be closer to her three brothers, Constantine, Matvei and Sergei, all who lived on the estate of Chornaya Graz. She wanted to return to the place where she spent some of her happiest times since their family's escape from Moldavia so long ago.

The crisp morning air of the lush green covered grounds of Chornaya Graz lingered throughout the estate and the hazy mist suspended from above the pond was beginning to clear. The edge of Maria's long crimson dress was damp from walking on the sparkling dew. She inhaled the fresh forestry scent and in a quick flash all the summertime memories of gone-by eras flooded her mind, as if waves crashing upon the shores of life. She leaned against one of the many white birch trees that were scattered through the estate grounds and began to weep. What was she going to do now? Her family was without a mother and without a father and she had lost her newborn and then her love. Life was cruel and merciless. There was no one to turn to, no one to ask for council in delicate manners of the mind.

Her father's wife, Anastasia Trubetskaya, was the same age, but lacked maturity. There was talk that she was attempting to get control of Chornaya Graz, claiming it was rightfully hers. The question of rightful ownership had been presented to the council for settlement. Documents, statements and various forms of evidence were on hand to support each claim. All were necessary, for Dmitri did not clearly state in his will who was to be the benefactor of his fortune. Dmitri's will stating that Antioch was the most promising of all the children was presented as evidence. Based on that declaration, Antioch was awarded the estate by the Empress. A suit brought on by Princess Trubetskaya challenged the ruling and the property was confiscated. Eventually, Antioch was victorious in the legal battle and all estates returned to him, but it caused his monetary resources to be exhausted.

Now, his brother Constantine disputed the ownership, leaving the matter in the hands of the supreme council to make a final decision in the family dispute. Chornaya Graz was transferred to Constantine Kantemir. The entire estate and fortune of ten thousand serfs were temporarily awarded to him.

Maria knew it was not a coincidence for Constantine was married to Princess Galitzine, whose father was Prince D.M. Golitsyn, a prominent member of the Supreme Secret Council. Maria intervened after the decision and suggested, although the property was in Constantine's name, it was still the Kantemir family estate and should be treated accordingly. The property was then peacefully divided between Constantine, Matvei and Sergei.

The brothers, satisfied with the judgment, immediately immersed themselves to further beautifying the landscape with architectural art, statues and fountains. A stone church replaced the wooden church dedicated to the icon of our *Lady Life-Giving Spring* and more festive gardens decorated the estate giving a park like appearance.

All were content with the decision of the supreme council and only Antioch felt he had been cheated. Although, the will did not specify an heir, all could see that he clearly was the one who excelled in education and studies as stated by their father. The document did not sway the greatly influenced council.

Antioch could do nothing, but accept the ruling in favor of Constantine. He did not have the desire to join his brothers at Chornaya Graz.

The pain of unfairness in his heart could not be erased for the estate with all its serfs should have been his. He would not dwell on what could not be changed; his disappointment and sorrows would be expressed in his satires. He accepted Maria's suggestion to take full time residence at Dmitri's palace in St. Petersburg. It would provide the solitude he so desired to continue with his learning and writings.

St. Petersburg's Academy of Sciences provided Antioch with the further education he so desired. He studied early Russian history with his father's secretary I. Fokerod and Professor G.S. Bayer. He wrote satires and compiled *"Simifonila Na Psaltyr,"* creative poetic verses dedicated to Catherine I in 1727. Several more poems and songs in syllabic verse followed. In spite of his youth, he began to be known as the most cultural and sophisticated young man of all Russia.

A bitter cold frost set in from the Arctic north and it blanketed 1729 St. Petersburg in glistening snow. On the bank overlooking the frozen Neva River stood the grand palace of Prince Antioch Dmitriyevich Kantemir. The backdrop of gray skies above the city highlighted its beauty and prominence. The three story stone edifice built by the great Italian architect, Francesco B. Rastrelli, blended into the silhouette of the tightly built-up Dvortsovaya Embankment. An unstoppable howling wind raced around the outer corners of the palace walls, intensifying the currents of crystal white snow that now concretely encircled the building, furthering a surreal storybook appearance. Illusions of steam appeared to rise from the deserted streets creating a mystical effect. The only sight of warmth was smoke rising from one of the chimneys in the far corner of the palace that held an opulent stucco facade balcony adorned with white pilasters and trim. It encased an elaborate carved arched window that rose from the floor to the ceiling. A candlelight sphere of yellow bluish lights illuminated the window, contrasting the darkened skies of winter.

A dark hovering figure was writing feverishly, and his shadow created a silhouette that distorted the pastel colors of the pink and yellow silk wall coverings of the room. His desk faced the fireplace, which earlier had been lit by the servants. Dressed in a blue brocade robe, his white powdered wig was of sharp contrast. Many hours later, only yellow and orange embers flickered in the hearth. Prince Antioch did not notice nor pay any attention to the darkness in the room. What he did notice was the sound of silence, as his thoughts scattered through the stillness of the night. That was the way he liked it: tranquility to stimulate the mind and his love for satirical works. An ominous foreshadowing was felt, overpowering and circling throughout, stopping only when joined with the creative forces that flowed throughout the room. He would write the words of bitter truth. He would awake the people about their ignorance, superstitions, and drunkenness—the main reasons for all calamities. He felt the ruling class should show a good example to the people. At present, the nobility was incapable of sensible business while simultaneously thinking themselves better than other classes.

Portentous thoughts, joining modest ones, created an understanding of the misunderstood. Prince Antioch would transpose that reflection on paper. With quill in hand, he continued to write until only remnants of ashes remained smoldering in the hearth.

To His Own Mind

O unripe mind, brief learning's fruit, be still!
Do not compel my hand to take the quill.
One cannot writing all one's day, find fame
And not possess an author's wide acclaim.
In our times many easy paths lead there.
On which bold steps can travel free of care.
Nine barefoot sisters traced the worst of all,
For many ere they reach it, fail and fall.
On it you have to sweat and pine away
While everyone avoids you like the plague,
And mocks and scorns you. He who sits alone,
Stares wide-eyed into books, will never own
Great places of garden statue-filled,
Nor will his father's flock the larger build.

Catherine I's reign did not last for long. Shortly after accession to the throne, she took ill and died of influenza. Princess Anna Ivanovna, daughter of Peter's half-brother Ivan was the new empress on the throne. She followed the principles of Peter the Great, but she was not a favorite with the people because she was cruel even by the standards of the time and was responsible for the deaths and exiles of many who opposed her regime. In cultural matters, she had the best interests of Russia at heart. She westernized and encouraged ballet and the arts. She had officers trained and created a cadet corps, the *Preobrazhensky* regiment in which Antioch enrolled as a young lieutenant. He hoped with the ascension of the new empress, his personal adversaries would be restored however; the empress was not interested in his plight. She had other plans for Antioch. He was appointed Russian ambassador to England.

It was a dark overcast day. The winds picked up and the snow began to fall steadily. Antioch was in a gloomy mood. His thoughts were on his pending trip to England. He walked over to his desk, stopping only briefly to look out the icicle-framed window. He could see the Peter and Paul Fortress in the distance. Its cathedral towered high into the sky with a huge cooper needle atop a golden spire, and with a gold angel that held a snow covered cross. He thought of Peter the Great who was buried at the cathedral yet, it was not so long ago, but then it seemed like an eternity, that he comforted his sister Maria at the eulogy of the Czar at the church. He hoped his satires would live forever, as would the Czar's greatness. He stared at the swirling snowflakes scurrying about the window, as if they were playing a game of tag. The various patterns of the snowflakes intrigued him. They seemed to be imitating the complexity of life's patterns, rising, falling and in an instant nonexistent. They were in an imbroglios state, as Antioch felt he was too. Was his life so different? One day it also would be nonexistent. A new maze of snowflakes flew past the window startling Antioch and obscuring his view of the fortress and the choppy gray waters of the Neva River. This new parade of snowflakes inspired him. It was a good day to write, a day to express his thoughts and emotions.

The lit fireplace warmed the darken room. A bitter cold frost set in from the Arctic north and soon it would bury St. Petersburg of 1729 in glistening snow. A candlelight sphere of yellow bluish lights illuminated on the writing paper. Antioch adjusted the white powdered wig on his head as he began to transpose fast and furious thoughts into words of satire on the sheet. He wrote four satires, dedicating the third to Feofan Prokopovich who in turn praised Antioch with a well-known epistle complimenting his satirical writings. Antioch's satires addressed the criteria for advancement on merit and ability rather than *'noble birth.'* His satires, mocked the clergy that had great influence on the positions of authority. They concentrated on the hypocrisies of Russia's social and political aspect and contained much information on the history of Russia, its literature and culture and the denouncements of corrupt noblemen. He wrote that noble, young Russian men sent abroad by Peter the Great to study and return to serve, instead were only interested in fashion of the day. His satires would open up the minds of the people and expose them to the truth.

Antioch's satires did not erase the pain of personal affairs. His outward appearance and the success of writings had hid his difficulties well. He was unhappy, discontent with the events caused by the uncertainty of his father's will. He confided in one person, the one closest to him, the one who shared his life since his birth, his sister, Maria. It was with her that he could divulge his candid feelings. She was the strong and sensible one. They had much in common for not only was Maria well educated and an intellect, she too had faced many of her own adversities, becoming stronger in the process. He was to leave soon for his new post as Russian Ambassador to England. He sent Maria a message informing her of his departure as he was hoping before his journey was to commence, he would see his sister. She had agreed to tend to his affairs and ensure all would be in order while he was abroad.

Maria's carriage pulled up in front of their *father's palace* as it was still called. The front rooms were aglow with light. Luggage sat outside the door of the building. The servants were scurrying about loading trunks that were to be transported to the ship that would sail for England. Antioch was inside, giving final instructions to the servants.

"This trunk is next," Maria heard him say as she entered through the open doorway.

"Antioch, I have arrived," said Maria running to give her brother a big hug.

"My, don't you look distinguished my dear brother! Have you prepared everything? What is in that big bag you are holding?" she asked looking at a heavy object in his hand.

"That is father's manuscript, *'History of the Growth and Decay of the Ottoman Empire.'* I will have it published in England. I shall write a biography of our father and add a bibliography to it. Father wrote it in Latin, finishing it in 1716. I acquired the services of a Mr. Tindal to assist me to translate it to English. Father's great works should not be forgotten," replied Antioch.

"Yes, of course. How, wonderful!" said Maria. "Antioch, don't forget your scarf. You will need it in the damp cold climate of England. I shall write to you and I expect you to also write and tell me all about your new life," continued Maria as she handed the scarf to Antioch. "Take care, my little brother and don't forget Princess Cherkasskaia. Write to your fiancé. I have done my best to arrange a marriage. The rest is up to you. We will wait for you and upon your return we shall have a splendid ceremony."

"Yes, sister, have no worries," replied Antioch.

The siblings exchanged hugs and kisses as the servants loaded the last trunk into the coach.

"*Dosvedaneya, moya sistra.* Good bye, my sister. When my work is finished abroad, I shall return and bring back all my new found knowledge and become President of the Academy of Sciences," shouted Antioch excitedly, waving his hand as the carriage rode off.

He was thrilled, yet sad to leave his country and family. It was January 1, 1732, a beginning of a new year, a new life in a new country. Antioch departed with high hopes and expectations. One day he would return with all that he had learned.

Cold vapors escaped from Maria's mouth as she blew a kiss to Antioch. It was a cold kiss and it was not a good sign. Maria shivered as the wind picked up. She pulled her wrap over her head and around her neck, not taking her eyes off the carriage that already was on its way around the bend and out of sight.

"Come back soon, my dearest brother," she said softly.

She returned to her waiting carriage as she was eager to return to courtyard life after a long absence. Empress Anna Ivanovna had invited her to be a lady in waiting. It would be a good opportunity to return to the social gaiety of arts, music and ballet in the royal court, but most importantly, she would then be in a better position to assist Antioch and oversee his progress in his new position as ambassador. He had just left and she was already missing him. She was looking forward to the day she would see her younger brother again.

Little did Maria know that her dreams would not come to be. Antioch would return to his motherland, but not alive.

21

The English Boy's Club

Antioch walked through the rooms of his home in the Golden Square *(Gelding Close)* district of London. The latest letter from Maria arrived today. He sat down at his writing desk and opened the letter. He was anxious to read it. The letter began with solid advice. "Do not allow anything serious to develop out of friendly kisses and conversations, and most importantly, that they not incur any unpleasantness and offend your fiancé."

Maria need not worry. With all the many presents I sent to Princess Cherkasskaia she should know the seriousness of my commitment to our relationship. Princess Cherkasskaia knows she is not forgotten and when I return to Russia I shall marry her. Princess Cherkasskaia is lady in waiting at the Empress's bedchamber. She is one of the richest young women in Russia and has a dowry of 70,000 serfs. I would not risk losing such a chance,' thought Antioch.

He hesitated a moment before continuing to read the letter and looked out the window. A light mist covered the greenery of the outdoor courtyard across the road from his home. Four garden squares covered the yard, two on each side. A row of trees, their branches bare from the steady rain surrounded the square. Dark rain clouds were scattered throughout the skies. From his view on the second floor Antioch could see rows of wet rooftops with their brick chimneys that lined the houses that surrounded Golden Square. Thirty-nine houses occupied the square that housed political and socially gentry. A great number of foreigners lived there, including many diplomatic envoys from other countries. Duchesses and dukes were its residents. Notable piano and harpsichord makers lived and worked in Golden Square.

A statue of the current king, George II stood in the center of the square. The statue was made for the Duke of Chandos in 1720 and had not yet officially been erected. It was only fitting his statue should grace the grounds of Golden Square for King George II was a great supporter of the Enlightenment movement. He was born outside of England, in Hanover Germany and spoke fluent German and French. He was open to the learned and permitted uncensored published works that helped pave the way for unlimited creativity. King George II granted sanctuary to Voltaire, when the philosopher was exiled from France. He was well liked by the foreign residents of his country, but unpopular with the English people due to his supposed inability to speak proper English.

Antioch felt very comfortable at No. 6 his home of five years as he had adjusted easily and was fond of this new foreign country with its unique ways that provided opportunities in all aspects of life. During his time in England he had accomplished much. There was harmony between the English and Russian government. He succeeded in sending an English ambassador to St. Petersburg, which helped with mutual talks and to establish agreements between the two countries. Czarina Anna Ivanovna was pleased and for his efforts he was given a promotion as extraordinary envoy. His personal endeavor was accomplished with the publications of his father's works. Dmitri Kantemir's *The History of the Growth and Decay of the Ottoman Empire*, was published in English in London in 1734. N. Tindal had successfully assisted with the translation of the original works from Latin into English.

Antioch continued to write satirical poems, among them a philosophical ode, *To a Malicious Person* in 1735. Although, stability between England and Russian had been established and his career was successful, his salary had not changed with his new title. His income was not sufficient enough to maintain the standard that was associated with such a position. His finances were exhausted. He had no choice, but to rely on his sister Maria for financial assistance.

Maria's latest letter informed him she was able to arrange a grant and a raise in his salary through her associates in St. Petersburg. Maria's much welcomed letter brought good news and relief. She made many contacts while hosting a literary salon in St. Petersburg. The salon gathering enabled guests to improve their intellect with discussions of literary works, philosophy and on occasion — gossip. Polite conversation prevailed throughout, following rules of etiquette, while exchanging thoughts and ideas that further enlightened those who attended. The literary salon became an institution popular among the thinkers. One of the letters from Maria told of *'les bas-bleus,'* the blue stockings — a nickname for the intellectual women that gathered in her literary salon.

The news of a grant put Antioch in a good mood. It would

allow him to send much needed material such as books and instruments to the Academy of Sciences in St. Petersburg and the increased income would lessen his financial burden.

Today, he would relax and enjoy the cosmopolitan atmosphere of London that he so admired. The social atmosphere of the city renewed Antioch's interests in opera and painting. England was a commercial nation with emphasis on trade and its prosperity provided opportunities for struggling artists. Antioch became a patron and an advocate of the arts. He had many friends which included fellow writers, composers, actors and actresses. He spent his leisure time with members of the diplomatic corps and highly educated men who too, took an interest in the sciences, literature and the arts. They called themselves a club, a *Boys Club*. Two of his closest artistic friends, the painter Jacopo Amigoni and the castrato singer Farinelli were members of the club.

Jacopo, an Italian painter of mythological works, was known for decorative and portraitist paintings. His paintings decorated the frescoes of many churches and palaces. He had just completed his latest work, *A Banquet of the Gods* on the ceiling of Covent Garden Theater and in the fresco above the stage. The mythological works were his best. Jacopo did portrait paintings as well and Antioch was so well pleased with the several that were done for him that he sent them on to St. Petersburg. Yes, he would invite Jacopo Amigoni to join him tonight.

"Ah," and then there was Farinelli. The magnetic Farinelli! He was an unusual tall Italian man, adorned by the people for his memorable arias. He became immensely famous throughout Italy and Europe for taking the female role in *'Sofonisba'* by Luc Antonio Predieri. He had come to London to sing. His soprano voice, was so enchanting that during his London debut performance of *'Artaxerxe,'* as Arbace, an ancient Persian hero, caused one Mrs. Fox-Labe to stand up and shout,

"One God! One Farinelli!" He had so charmed the ladies that they became overcome with emotion on hearing his beautiful soprano voice. They were captivated with this charming castrated half man, half God like creature who had a hypnotic effect upon them. Men, also were fascinated with the presence of this unique creature of a person, making him an instant success with the public.

The three men complemented each other's style and used one another to promote themselves. Jacopo painted two portraits of Farinelli. One full portrait showed the muse of music, *'Euterpe'* crowning Farinelli. It was a regal painting for the tall man with a protruding upper lip, and an unusual physic and abnormal round huge chest. Farinelli in turn, was a patron of Jacopo and it was Jacopo who had introduced Farinelli to Antioch. The relationship among the three proved to be an advantage.

Antioch found Farinelli pleasant, entertaining and culturally pleasing. He would complete the threesome for dinner at their favorite tavern, the *"Crow and Lion"* located near Covent Gardens. Perhaps, after dinner they would see a ballet at the theater. Antioch made arrangements to meet them tonight to celebrate the wonderful news of his good fortune, but first he would have a cup of tea. The damp weather put him in the mood to try the latest tea he purchased at Twining on Strand. Thomas Twining sold the finest teas in London and Antioch especially was fond of exotic teas from east India. He would try the *Assam* tea, a full-bodied tea with a malt flavor, which was not yet introduced to the public. Twining had limited quantities and sought Antioch's opinion before he would proceed to sell it in his store. Antioch breathed in the vapors of the strong black tea as he drank. Yes, this tea would get his approval.

The *Crow and Lion* tavern was noisy and crowded as Antioch entered. He made his way past artists, musicians, dancers, composers, set designers, and patrons of the art world.

My, what a motley group of people, all uniquely dressed in various styles and clothing, carrying on conversations that only an artist from an artist world would understand. They are totally engrossed in their talks and untouched by reality, thought Antioch.

He noticed Jacopo and Farinelli seated at a blue velvet draped table, the one in the far corner of the tavern.

"Sorry, I am late. My carriage took a wrong turn in this foggy weather," said Antioch pulling out a chair.

"You made it safely and that is most important. We hope you don't mind, we took the liberty of ordering a bottle of French cognac while awaiting you. Here, sit down and let us make a toast, before we begin our meal," said Farinelli picking up his glass.

This is going to be a festive and interesting evening as it always is whenever we get together, thought Antioch.

"Cheers, to our good health. Drink up, gentlemen," began Jacopo.

The three men quickly gulped down their first glass of cognac.

"Now, we can enjoy the remainder of the evening," said Farinelli as he continued to pour more cognac into the empty glasses.

Jacopo turned to Antioch who was busy spreading caviar on his bread.

"Antioch, how honored are we that you have chosen us to share in your good news. The *Academy of Sciences* will well benefit from the grant graciously arranged by your sister. It all shall be waiting for you when you return to your country."

"Yes, Maria was able to convince the Empress and since, I have been so successful in England, I was hoping the Empress will allow me to return home soon. Upon my return to Russia, I shall live a quiet prosperous life, with only a few chosen friends such as you and Farinelli. I prefer a calm life a midst *dead Greeks and Romans*, opposed to the noisy life of political activities of *hypocrisy, cruelty and trampling of human dignity*. Do not forget gentlemen, my ancestors sat on the throne of the Eastern Holy Roman Empire. Those are my thoughts for the evening, gentlemen," Antioch concluded as he looked about the tavern.

His attention was caught by music coming from a harpsichord from the front room of the darken tavern. He reminisced of his sister Maria playing the harpsichord for what seemed like not so long ago. He strained his neck to follow the flow of notes until his eyes stopped on a focal vision, the very core of the blissful melody. A young lady with dark hair, in the palest blue transparent dress was at the keys of the wooden harpsichord. A pearl ornament decorated her low bodice, exposing just the top of her well-rounded breasts. A matching pearl band held her curly hair that was piled high on top of her head. Two candelabras on the piano were all aglow, partially lighting up the front of the tavern. Antioch could not help, but notice that the young lady's incandescent beautiful blue eyes were lost in the melody of the music. It was only her and her music. No one was able to enter the world of a musician once they were entranced in their own song. Antioch sensed this as he had seen it before, in Maria's music. He noticed Jacopo and Farinelli also strained to see and hear the sounds of music, which had turned to a malleable melody.

"Ah, all true artists are sent here from heaven. Let us not forget where we came from. No doubt, this young lady was at the front of the line. We are only instruments of which came from above," said Farinelli.

"Farinelli, you can make anyone forget their troubles with your philosophy of life," said Jacopo.

"Yes, eloquently said," added Antioch.

"Pardon sir, your meals are here," said the waiter as he carefully placed each dish in front of his customers.

The aroma of steak and kidney pie interrupted the philosophical mood, bringing the *'Boys Club'* back to reality, but not before Antioch could make an announcement.

"My, dear friends, I have an ulterior motive for inviting you to dinner tonight. Yes, it is to celebrate the good news of a grant, but there is something more important you should know. I have also received news from St. Petersburg that I have been reassigned as Russian ambassador to France. My new post begins September 8, 1738 and I shall be leaving soon."

Jacopo and Farinelli both let out a gasp. They did not expect to be separated at this time of their lives when they were all at the height of their success and so instrumental to one another.

"Antioch, what can we say? We wish you all the best and we will surely miss you. I will continue to correspond with you Antioch, as we always had before. That will not change. It is unfortunate however, that you will not be returning to Russia sooner as was anticipated," said Jacopo.

"Yes, it was a disappointment, gentlemen, but tonight we shall enjoy the flavors of friendship as one enjoys the nectar of flowers. Gentlemen, let us savor this evening and enjoy the best that London has to offer for tomorrow is another day and can never replace today," added Antioch.

"Speaking of sweet nectar, Marie Salle is dancing this evening in the ballet, *Caracteres de le Danse* at the Covent Theatre. One never knows what artistic styles she has developed lately. She dances dramatically and elegantly. She has her own thoughts on dance and with competition from Marie Camargo it will prove to be an interesting evening. One will never forget her grace of dance and the scandal of her costume: simple dress, no skirt, only a one piece bodice and her hair down. She is not only a creature of creativity; she is of quick mind and intelligence. Marie Salle expresses herself through dance with thoughts of the mind and that makes her a unique mortal," said Antioch.

"Yes, she can certainly rival the perfections of Marie Camargo's entrechats. Each time a Marie dances, one is more exquisite than the other," replied Jacapo. "Voltaire was correct when he stated, 'Ah! Camargo. How brilliant you are! But, great gods, how ravishing is also Salle.'"

"Yes, a ballet is in order after dinner," said Antioch, his mind drifting back to the music in the tavern.

With dinner completed, the men gathered their belongings to leave the *Crow and Lion* tavern and headed for the ballet at the Covent. As Antioch exited, he exchanged glances with the young lady who had lifted her head from the keys of the harpsichord as she finished her last piece. She smiled shyly at Antioch's glance. Antioch became smitten and instantly felt much younger than his years. The young lady lowered her head back to her keyboard, causing a lock of her curly hair to fall delicately on her forehead.

"Ah, she can make me easily forget my fiancé Princess Cherkassikaia," whispered Antioch to Jacapo, forgetting his promise to Maria not to offend his fiancé.

"What difference could it make, she is there and you are here and that is the fact of life, perhaps a ménage a trois," said Farinelli with a smile.

"Non, jaurai des maitresses," answered Antioch and then quickly added. "Gentlemen and I mean gentlemen, enough with the antidotes. A ballet is waiting for us!"

As the *Boys Club* left the tavern, Antioch turned his head back for one more look at the young damsel and thought, *'Perhaps I shall return, another time, to continue the unfinished.'*

The English Boy's Club | 199

22

Paris, 1738–1744

Paris, so different and distinct from London, was a city of gaiety, amusement and a place Antioch longed to visit. To his disappointment, the city was not what he had envisioned. The Parisian alderman, Thomas Germain was there to welcome Antioch when he first arrived. He assisted Antioch in making the transition and introducing him to the aspects of Parisian life, but it did not help. Antioch found the city atmosphere mistrustful of him as a foreigner. It was further complicated by the Parisian's dislike of Russia. Among all the animosity, it was difficult for Antioch to retain peaceful conditions between the two countries. Recent unexplained circumstances arose which made Antioch further suspicious of the French government and their intentions. One of the aspects of cultural life in Paris as an ambassador was to take part in card games. Antioch found the endless games of cards fruitless, but he was obliged to participate.

It was one such evening, that Antioch walked through the streets of Paris to attend a game of cards. He was feeling unhappy, as he preferred not to attend such a function. As he passed along a few buildings he caught glimpses of dark shadowy figures and thought he heard footsteps from behind. He turned his head, but saw nothing.

"Ah, this government is playing tricks with me. They can follow me all they want. They will find me boring just as I find them. I only look forward to the day I can return home," muttered Antioch.

The faster he walked to attend the card game, the faster this unproductive evening would be over. He walked briskly until he reached his destination.

"Ah, the Russian Ambassador has final arrived," exclaimed Thomas Germain opening the door.

He led Antioch to the library. Its wooden floors were covered with red area rugs and had floor to ceiling burgundy draped windows that made the room appear smaller than it was. Its wall-to-wall shelves were covered entirely with dark leather bounded books. A chandelier hung from a trey ceiling in the center of the room above a table where the guests gathered. It provided the only light in the hazy room.

The mood of this room reflects my feelings of Paris. A city sparkling with the effervescence of a glittering life, yet dim murky microscopic shadows of distrust and uncertainty creep about, was the thought running through Antioch's mind.

"Ambassador Kantemir, we have been waiting for you. We have started to play without you. Your deck of cards is there. You still have time to join us," continued Thomas, pointing to the table.

Antioch took off his cloak, hung it on one of the wall knobs and sat down at the round wooden table. He glanced at the five gentlemen around him and saw that they were engrossed with the cards in their hands and they did not pay any attention to him, except for one gentleman, the gentleman still wearing an evening cloak with dampness on the shoulders. It appeared the man had just arrived and was in a rush to play cards and had forgotten to remove his wrap. He was studying his deck of cards, yet he seemed to be focused on Antioch as well.

"I see we have a new friend joining us this evening," said Antioch.

The gentleman looked up for a moment without replying and then returned to concentrate on his deck of cards.

"Gentlemen, I have won once more!" exclaimed Thomas. He flung his cards face up in the center of the table.

"What an impromptu moment. Congratulations Thomas," replied Antioch staring at the deck of aces suspiciously.

I'll join them in their little game of charade. After all, being an ambassador all these years taught me how to skillfully participate in the learned art of pretense, thought Antioch.

"Now, that the game is over, I hope you will give me an opportunity to view some of your silver-works, Thomas," said Antioch continuing with his charade. "I would like to take some pieces back to Russia upon completion of my assignment. My sister, Maria would be pleased at such an exquisite gift of your making. I was thinking perhaps, a silver tea set or a fine *surtout de table* (centerpiece) would be an ideal gift."

"It will be my pleasure. My workshop has made many objects for the Portuguese court and I will be most honored to do the same for the Russian court," replied Thomas.

"Gentlemen, I must depart," interrupted the stranger still wearing his cloak.

"Must you leave so soon? We had not had an opportunity to be properly introduced," said Antioch.

The stranger remained silent, ignoring Antioch's request. He turned his back to all.

"Avoir, my friends," were the only words uttered as he left.

"Strange fellow," said Thomas.

Antioch too felt puzzled by this man whose intentions he found quite questionable, but it did not surprise him as it was just one of many similar occurrences during his time in Paris. He thought he had gotten accustomed to such infringements, but continued to be exasperated when they occurred. The constant trickery of on-going intrigue for reasons unknown began to strain him mentally and physically. His felt his suspicions of being followed were in fact a reality and difficult to ignore. It was *videre* (evident) as Antioch would say later. "Videre, videre," were the words he liked to repeat when such happenings occurred.

Unknown to Antioch, all these unexplained episodes were part of a plot to force him out of France. During his time in Paris, Antioch did not write to Jacopo or his friends as he had promised. He missed England. He missed his mother country and his family. He found life in Paris under these uncertain circumstances oppressive. His assignment in France was not as short as Antioch had hoped. Only the correspondences between himself and Maria kept him sane. He enjoyed and took pleasure in her letters for she kept him abreast of all the current political and social events in Russia.

Much time passed since his departure from Russia and Antioch developed new interests as he lost old ones, one of them being Princess Varvara Alekseyevna Cherkasskaia. She had written him with an ultimatum that she could wait no longer for him. He had to make a decision, a commitment to marry immediately. Antioch finished reading the letter. He was not surprised for he expected this moment to come and he dreaded it. He did not like being put in this position and be forced to make a decision he was uncertain of.

He was not prepared to commit to the princess or to anyone. He knew not when, if ever, he would be ready, even if love did find its way to him, for he felt restricted by its demand. He would not entrust his being to a single person! Antioch was torn between the thought of losing the wealthy Princess Cherkasskaia and of doing what was right for himself. To marry, would be a prison sentence for someone like him. He felt faint and sick with the realization of what must be done. He would not marry.

The Princess's letter fell out of his hand and landed on the floor. Without thought, he punched the wall with his fist creating a large hole. Bits of plaster and dust tumbled down. His bruised knuckles swelled with redness. He walked to the wash closet and vomited. He took a cloth from the wash basin, dipped it in cool water and wiped his face. He looked at himself in the mirror.

"No, I will not change my mind," he said to the reflection.

Accepting the fact of a broken relationship, Antioch decided to write to Maria. He began with, "As far as the tigress is concerned, I no longer think about her at all. I am so fed up with these never-ending, fruitless conversations about her that I have lost all patience with them."

Shortly after, another letter arrived from Maria. Princess Cherkasskaia, upon word that Antioch had broken their engagement, immediately received a proposal of marriage from Count Peter Sheremetev. Her mass fortune had helped her find another suitor.

With the matter settled, Antioch could focus on more important issues such as his writings, diplomatic work and continued friendship with Voltaire who thanked Antioch for the use of his father's work of *The History and Decay of the Ottoman Empire*. Two additional editions of the works were published in Paris in 1743 and widely received. A biography of Dmitri Kantemir, which Antioch wrote, was included in the French editions.

During Antioch's time in Paris, a new Empress had come to rule Russia. Elizabeth Petrovna was the daughter of Peter the Great and his wife Catherine I. She had finally found her place on the throne. Once more rumors were circulating that Antioch would be recalled home. Antioch was in agony, living a life of uncertainty. Once again he wrote to Maria. He wanted to return to live with her and his brothers, *"even if poorly, but on the other hand in peace."* The dream of becoming the President of the Academy of Sciences never wavered from his mind. It was one of the few things that sustained him during the turmoil times of Paris; the other, letters and gifts exchanged with Maria. Antioch sent Maria thirteen Italian books in addition to books based on astrology and geometry, which she had requested.

"I find pleasure in your books. It is an escape from the bores of everyday house chores. It stimulates the mind; to learn and to gain knowledge is endless. One does not want to be stupid one's entire life. You can add that thought to your satires, Antioch," wrote Maria. "Furthermore, since the 1737 fire in my home where I was left without bed and lost many belongings, I realize the importance of knowledge, not material things that vanish into air. I am much satisfied with my rebuilt Moscow home, which I have named *New Ark* and I have my cats and dogs. They give me much solace as do my books and helping the poor. My reflection of life is such that I wish to do good will. Now, my brother, I turn to you for serious advice: I am considering entering a monastery, to pray to God, to give to the church and to help the needy. Please respond to me with your candor thoughts. I anxiously await your reply," signed, your loving sister, Maria.

Several months passed before a reply was received from Antioch.

"I beg you not to think of this matter to enter a monastery any further. I wish that when I return home, you could live your entire life together with me, in my home, being the mistress of the house greeting and entertaining guests. We will be each other's strength. I wish that you would find pleasure and happiness in such a way of life. I look forward to returning home to you, my brothers, and the place where our parents remains rest. I have always wanted to visit Paris. Now, I am here enjoying all manner of life's comfort, but nonetheless can hardly wait for the hour when I shall get out of here," your beloved brother, Antioch.

Maria knew Antioch provided sound advice for her as she had done for him. She made preparations for his anticipated return to Russia; however, unknown to Maria, Antioch was seriously ill. He took to the waters of *Aix-en-Provence and Plombieres* to relieve the pain that plagued him. The waters did not help for the pain was worsening. There was only one option. He would have to travel to Italy for treatment. He wrote in tears to Empress Elizabeth to allow him to travel to Italy and for a medical allowance. Empress Elizabeth had granted permission, but it was without an allowance and it arrived too late. Antioch was in agony and in critical condition. He was unable to travel. Before Maria could reply to her brother's last letter, a white envelope trimmed with a black border arrived from Paris. Maria's hand trembled as she opened it.

The letter began... "It is with deep regret we inform you the death of the Russian ambassador to France, his honorable Prince Antioch Dmitrivich Kantemir on March 31,

1744. Please accept our deepest sympathy and condolences."
Sincerely yours, Jean-Jacques Amelot de Chaiilou, French
Foreign Minister.

23

Chornaya Graz — the Final Years

Despite her grief-stricken state, Maria knew what had to be done. Antioch's remains would come home. She would make all the necessary arrangements and ask the Empress to help return her brother's remains to Russian. However, it seemed neither the Empress nor the Russian government paid any attention. The Russia government's relationship with Antioch had been strained as a result of his works and ties with controversial figures such as Voltaire and Montesquieu. As a diplomat he had profound knowledge and the skill of international relations, handling the complex situation of the '*War for the Austrian Succession*' from 1740-1744. His diplomatic correspondences contained an in-depth analysis of the foreign policies of European States and his prestige in their capitals made the Czarist government tolerate his services.

Maria waited, but there was no response from the Russian government. She had no choice, but to borrow money and get into debt to have Antioch returned home. His body was transported back to Russia and buried in Moscow in the church of the Greek *'Nikolsky Monastery,'* alongside his father Prince Dmitri Kantemir, his mother Princess Cassandra Cantacuzene and his sister Princess Smaragda I. His surviving brothers, Matvei, Sergei and Constantine, ordered that Antioch's books be sold in Paris and that only original works and translations of their brother be forwarded to them. Although, his life and death was ignored by the Russian government, his satires were the beginning of Russian classicism and literature.

Emptiness filled Princess Maria's days. With those closest to her gone there was a void in her life. She decided living spiritually and giving to those less fortunate would fill that void and she began to devote her time to the church and helping the poor. With Antioch's untimely death in mind, Maria prepared a will, that with her death, 1,000 rubles should go to construction of a monastery at her home and 3,000 rubles for its upkeep and that the monastery should have 12 monastic monks. Her two estates, and a home in Moscow and an expensive service set that Antioch had gifted her from abroad should go to the monastery. If construction of such a monastery was not authorized, her money should go to the poor and offerings should be made to build a church.

Satisfied her affairs were in order Maria decided to take a ride to the countryside, to Chornaya Graz to visit her remaining surviving brothers.

"Natasha, prepare my belongings. I am going away to Chornaya Graz. It will do me good. The estate is my comfort. Being there, even in my darkest times has always calmed me. Please have the driver bring the carriage to the front. The day is perfect for such a trip," she said to the housekeeper.

Maria looked out the window. The sunny blue skies lighten

her mood. She took a brush from her dressing table and brushed her long brown hair. She gathered it on top of her head, in an up-sweep and pinned two crystal blue combs into place. They matched the blue dress she wore. A long mink coat completed her look. She scurried down the long winding stairway and into the mirrored foyer with its large chandelier. The many spectrums of colors from the chandelier gave the small room a luxurious appearance. Maria glanced in the mirror as she passed, pushing her locks in place with her hand.

The trunks Natasha had prepared were waiting for her at the doorstep. She recalled Antioch's trunks outside the door of the Neva Palace when she bide him *adieu* before his departure for England. It seemed so long ago.

Yes, it is a good idea to spend some time with my brothers, she affirmed as she walked out the door and into the waiting carriage. She covered her lap with a blanket and placed her hands into a matching hand mitt. She was anxious to get started.

"Coachman, please put the top cover of the carriage down. I would like to get some fresh air on this beautiful day," she said.

"Yes, Madame, but first the horses need water. It'll only be a few more minutes," he answered, putting her trunks into the rear of the carriage.

Once all was done, the driver cracked his whip, a signal for the horses to begin their gallop. However, something went terribly wrong. Without warning, the horses angered by the force of the whip, turned their gallop into a run. It was a fast run the driver could not control. The horses with the carriage occupants sped into the main road.

"Whoa! Whoa! Stop! Stop!" shouted the driver.

He could not control the powerful horses. Maria held on to the sides of the carriage, frozen with fear as they continued their furious run. Maria screamed. The horses did not slow down when they approached a pending curve. The carriage flipped over landing upside down, its two rear wheels spinning as it came to a halt. A blanket lay besides the carriage; two crystal blue combs sparkled nearby on the cold street. A passing carriage slowed to take a look at the crash scene and then continued on its way, crushing the two blue combs into splinters. Maria could not be seen. She was pinned beneath the carriage.

"Help, help," shouted the driver who managed to jump from the carriage before the crash.

People came running and gathered around the accident site. A few burly men helped the driver lift the carriage. Maria lay still, not breathing. Her face was white. She had been killed instantly. No sooner than five minutes had elapsed since she left her home. It was Sept. 9, 1754.

Maria was 54 years old. It was one month after the signing of her will.

Only a few close friends attended Maria's funeral. Matvei and Sergei her two surviving brothers, stated that due to health issues, they were unable to travel to St. Petersburg for her funeral. Housekeeper Natasha, standing in the rear of the church strained to look at the coffin containing her mistress's remains, as the many rows of black hats blocked her view. She was grief-stricken, sobbing quietly as she remembered how well treated she was by the princess.

"I shall never forget her kindness, or her sadness," said Natasha, trying to console herself. "May the princess rest in peace, for she has joined her love. Maria and Peter, the great love affair of the 1700's."

Matvei and Sergei did not fulfill Maria's last will and wishes. They did not distribute her money to the building of a monastery or give to the church or the poor. Instead, shortly thereafter, they split Maria's money among themselves. The only wish they did follow was to bury Princess Maria next to her beloved brother, Antioch, their sister Smaragda and their father and mother at the *Nikolsky Greek* Cemetery in Moscow.

Matvei Kantemir used the funds from Maria's will to further beautify the grounds of Chornaya Graz. A greenhouse was built to cultivate fruits and citrus trees. The *Our Lady of Life-Giving Spring* church was enlarged and rebuilt. A new stone dining hall and a two level bell towers were added. Vibrant flower and fruit gardens were replanted. Lush green ivy edges surrounded Kantemirovka, the pergola on the nearby hill, *a patina among the many birch trees on the estate.*

Matvei and Sergei Kantemir lived peacefully at Chornaya Graz until 1771 when Matvei died. Only Sergei was left. Without Maria and without any family's guidance, Sergei became irresponsible. He took to gambling and lost most of what he took from Maria's fortune. He lost his own fortune as well in a dangerous card game known as *Varaon*. He could not keep away from the popular card game. It would only be a matter of time, before he would lose all, including *Chornaya Graz* to his addiction. Through the intervention of Catherine the Great, Sergei was able to eventually get out of debt, for she prohibited such dangerous gambling games and saved Sergei from further ruin.

Summer of 1777. Catherine the Great was visiting Chornaya Graz with the Russian general and statesman, Griogory Potemkin. He was the current favorite of Catherine and he was her lover. She had spent a few summers at the estate, as a guest of Sergei. She loved the grounds and her time spent there with Potemkin. She appreciated the beauty of the many ponds and streams on the grounds, its sunny gardens and shady groves.

Her romance with Potemkin blossomed among the splendor of the outdoors during that time. She could not do without Chornaya Graz. She had to own it. She would approach Sergei Kantemir with an offer.

"My dear, Prince Sergei Dmitrivich, why do you need this estate? You are old and getting older. And your funds are almost depleted and you cannot take the proper care of *'Chronaya Graz'* that it deserves. It is a paradise and should be kept that way. Let me help you. Allow me to purchase the estate. I will pay you grandly, a sum of 25,000 rubles. Please consider my generous offer seriously."

"Your, royal highness, your offer requires much thought. This estate has been my family home for over 60 years and the grounds hold many memories for me. I need time to consider what you are proposing," replied Sergei.

"Very well, but do not take my offer lightly," answered Catherine.

Sergei knew Catherine was right, but in his heart he was tormented. How could he give up his family's home, the only home he has known since the move from Moldavia? All the memories, the good times, the bad times, all belonged to Chornaya Graz. Years of memories locked in every flower, every tree. The life and death of each Kantemir cascading with the flow of the streams on the grounds.

Memories could not be erased. Sergei felt weak and helpless as he sat under the big fig tree, the one that he helped his brother Matvei plant. He put his hands to his face and began to cry. He was 70 years old. Life had come and soon it will leave. He was forced to make a decision. He would sell Chornaya Graz to Catherine the Great. With heavy heart, Sergei reluctantly conceded the property to Catherine the Great.

"Ahh, I have great plans for this glorious estate. It is my utopia, my *Tsaritsyno*. I will rename it just that. I cannot wait to get started. I already have an architect in mind to mold the estate into a more stylish form," said Catherine upon learning of Sergei's decision.

"You mean you will not be employing the court architect, Rastrelli?" asked Potemkin.

"No, not at all, I have the architect Visily Bazhenov in mind. I prefer the Gothic style with pavilions for my plan. Rastrelli and his baroque are no longer fashionable. I have no need for his services. Please arrange one of my advisers to inform him," said Catherine as she threw her head upwards, fanning her face with her hand as she walked away happily repeating '*Tsaritsyno, Tsaritsyno*' as the winds picked up, swirling the leaves from the estate in circles and propelling Chornaya Graz three hundred years later and to the year 1967.

My thoughts snapped back to reality and to the tour guide who was completing her narrative of the past.

"His talents are eternally encrusted in the Russian Maritime Headquarters in St. Petersburg, the Cathedral of the Resurrection near Moscow, and St. Andrew's church in Kiev. Rastrelli's designs were ignored and discarded, trashed and forgotten for he was no longer a court architect and his life as a once great architect was gone, along with the baroque. He pleaded with Catherine the Great to give him and his family an allowance to allow them to survive. It was finally with reluctance that Catherine agreed. Francesco Rastrelli, who lived fifty of his seventy one years in Russia, who had gained fame and honor, lived the last years of his life near poverty. His architectural designs disappeared, as did he. Even the exact date of his death and place of his grave is not known," said the guide sympathetically.

"After all, an architect is valued here only when he is needed, Rastrelli would like to repeat in the later years of his life," she concluded.

Chornaya Graz — the Final Years | 215

"My, I was so engrossed in my own thoughts and stories of what this place would have been like so many hundreds of years ago. How something so old could survive and yet look so magnificent is amazing," I blurted out to the guide as I walked about admiring the landscape.

"You speak and walk as if the grounds belong to you," replied the guide.

"Yes, I feel as if it does. I have much to tell my father of this trip when I return home to America."

Little did I imagine that years later it would be papa revealing much of what I had unwittingly experienced.

24

Winter in Connecticut — 1971

W inter arrived earlier than expected. I was engrossed with the visual display of the snowflakes that rested on the outer edges of the living room window. A gust of wind came along and scooped them up, blowing them into swirling circles. The many trees that lined 49 Silver Street where I now lived were crystallized with ice and the roads were blanketed with snow, causing the few cars that ventured out to slush the pallid substance onto the sidewalk. It was not a good day to be out. Taking an apple from a nearby bowl, I curled up on the sofa for as a young girl I liked to munch while reading and, at the time was deeply engrossed in a *Nancy Drew* mystery book when papa entered the room.

"Ella, one of our ancestors is a Russian poet. Here is an article about him in the *Novy Russky Slovo* newspaper," he said.

I glanced up from the pages of my book to look at the article in papa's hand. It did not impress me as it could not be that important for such a tiny piece. *How can a poet of any stature have such a small article written about him,* I thought, shrugging off his words and returning to my reading.

"Look, Ella. He was a poet in the 1700's," continued papa.

"What? We can trace our ancestor to 1700, such a long time ago, wow! Tell me more, papa," I said, putting my book aside, more impressed that an ancestor could be traced so far back, than the fact that he was well known. I looked at the short article that was printed in Russian as papa began to read aloud: *"A.D. Kantemir (1708-1744) famous determined writer, founder of satirical literature."*

The article was dated November 19, 1971.

"Is that all, Papa?" I asked, disappointed that there seemed to be no more written about our ancestor.

"Antioch Kantemir has written many poetic satires. He also has noble blood," continued papa.

"If he is related to us, then is he the connection to our noble blood that you once stated," I questioned.

"Yes," replied papa.

I resumed my reading, more impressed with a discovery of a 16th century ancestor than the fact that Antioch Kantemir was an accomplished poet.

In a matter of minutes the sound of strange exotic music filled the room. Papa had put a record on the phonograph and was dancing outlandishly. His arms were outstretched, his upper chest shaking and quivering.

'What has gotten into papa?' I wondered. I had never seen this style of dance. It was unrecognizable and foreign. I never knew that papa had such talent and it astonished me.

"Papa, where did you ever learn to dance like that?" I asked him.

"My grandfather Gregory Kantemir taught me and his grandfather taught him. It's a Turkish dance. Let me show you," he said continuing to dance about the room.

I jumped up and tried to mimic papa's upper body motions, but could not. I was too rigid from all my ballet training. Papa seemed to be skilled in this form of dance and apparently had expert training. Frustrated, I could only sit down to watch papa's Turkish dance. At the conclusion of his dance, strange sounds came from his mouth. He was speaking a language I had never heard before.

"What language is that?" I asked.

"It is Greek," he replied.

"Papa, where did you learn to speak Greek? You have never been to Greece. You have never been to Turkey. Did your grandfather teach you Greek too? Had he been to those countries?" I further inquired.

"No, my daughter, my grandfather Gregory taught me, as his grandfather taught him and I shall teach you," he answered.

I laughed as papa as continued to speak Greek. I had known papa to speak only Russian and very broken English. Now, I was hearing this strange and new language and I was enjoying the unusual moment with him. He was unleashing some of the past and its secrets.

"I will tell you one more thing that before I left Russia, I buried a bag filled with gold coins and jewelry. It was a velvet purple bag tied with a silver ribbon. The contents are very, very old. I buried the bag in the ground, next to a wall near a fence and beneath a tree, in the town of Cherkessk, Russia. I remember the location precisely, as if I had buried it yesterday. One day I hope it can be recovered by you or your siblings," papa continued.

"Papa, how can I ever find that gold filled bag? It is impossible. After all this time, a new building may stand on that place. It will never be found," I replied disappointingly.

"You can find it because it is buried beneath a very special tree, a birch tree like no other, the 'queen of the woods,' an enchanting tree, both beautiful and graceful. It is a tall birch with white bark and black carved lace-like markings that reach into each branch. I even carved my initials 'BIK' on the trunk. The beriozka, the tree of life, is waiting for a Kantemir to reclaim the contents which it has been guarding ever since," papa exclaimed positively.

"No, papa, It seems impossible," I said.

My discouraging remark seemed to change papa's mood and he returned silently to his room, clutching the newspaper article in his hand. It was another out of the ordinary conversation with papa however, to my surprise a few days later he approached me with the same article in his hand.

"I have something for you. I have saved this article on our ancestor and typed some words below it. I want you to keep it."

"Why should I save this article, Papa? What has it got to do with me?" I asked taken aback by his statement.

"You will need it. Just take it. One day you will need to prove who you really are," he replied.

"Papa, why would I have to prove who I am, to whom? No one is interested and no one cares what happened 300 years ago," I commented.

Never the less, I accepted the article from papa. The clipping was outlined in a green marker and was pasted on a yellow piece of paper. In Russian, and beneath the article, papa typed; *"Ella, this is the surname of your great-great-great-grandfather on the male bloodline, on the bloodline of your father — me, Boris Kantemir 22/ IX — 1971 year."* It ended with papa's signature: Boris Kantemir.

"Our name Kantemir has a special meaning. Translated in Tatar, *Kan* means blood, *Temir* mean iron or, 'Iron Blood,' he said.

Puzzled by the entire scenario, I took the document that papa had prepared and put it in my desk. I did not think too much of the article that lay in my desk for decades. That is until an occasion arose for me to present proof of my ancestry. Luckily, papa had the foresight and that I had listened.

January 1982. Boris Ivanovich Kantemir was calm as he walked to New Britain General Hospital. The pain on the right side of his abdomen was getting worse, but he was not too worried. The hospital was close to his home. He knew exactly what the problem was. He researched the symptoms in a medical book that he kept at home, on top of the many stacks of newspapers in his room. Anytime, he got a pain he would check his book. This time, he made a diagnosis of appendicitis. He would not waste time to go to Dr. Bolenski's office. Instead, he made the decision to walk the short distance to the hospital. He knew he had to have an immediate operation so he phoned the doctor to let him know that he was on the way to the hospital and would meet him there. Dr. Bolenski was already waiting at the main entrance when Boris arrived. The doctor, along with other physicians confirmed the diagnosis.

"Call my wife. She is at work. Please let her know the situation and that I am here," Boris said.

Dr. Bolenski placed a call to Dina, Boris's wife and reassured her of the simple procedure that was to take place.

"It is nothing to be anxious about. Removing an appendix is a normal routine for the medical profession. The operation itself, will not take more than a few hours. You need not be there. By the time you finish your work shift, the operation will be over and your husband will be good as new."

"We will call you once the operation is completed," Dina heard another voice say from the background.

Boris looked anxiously about as he was being prepared for the operation. From his angle, he could see his abdomen being scrubbed down with an orange colored antiseptic and the area being covered with a white sheet. A light-blue cotton net was placed over his hair. He could barely make out the face that administered the anesthesia that would soon put him to sleep. His eyes became heavy. He thought he saw his wife looking down at him and smiling. He could feel her caress on his hand. She had come after all. He would be in good hands. With a faint smile on his face, Boris drifted off into an unconscious state.

A series of unexpected prolonged sounds that no one liked to hear was heard throughout the hospital corridor.

"Beep, beep, beep."

Code three was the signal of a patient in distress and it was coming from the operating room. Emergency personnel ran through the hospital halls and pushed the doors open. Not a moment was to be wasted for the patient was in cardiac arrest.

"Stand back!" shouted Dr. Bolenski as paddles of electricity were applied to the patient's chest.

"Again, again again," shouted another doctor.

The body bounced up and down from the shock of electricity. They were losing the patient fast. Once more the paddles were applied, but it did not help. The series of beeps on the monitor became one long one. It was hopeless. The patient could not be saved and was declared deceased. Nothing could be done to bring him back. A white sheet was pulled over Boris Kantemir.

"What? The doctors told me not to come. When I did, they told me to leave. They said it was a simple operation. I held his hand. I reassured him all would be fine. Go back to work, don't worry they said, and now, my husband is dead! How could he die before the operation even started? How could that be? Was it the anesthesia? I demand an explanation! I need to know what happened," cried Dina, who had now become a widow.

Dr. Bolenski had no explanation for he was perplexed himself. The medical staff was lost for words. The only account came from an unknown assisting doctor, who was completing the final paperwork.

"The thought of a pending operation had further weakened your husband's unstable heart causing a heart attack," was his justification to the family members.

His explanation was puzzling, in fact the entire scenario was puzzling and the circumstances were certainly suspicious.

When, informed of papa's passing, I remembered his words, nineteen years earlier when Nicholas was killed in the crane accident. *If I died in an accident, it would not be an accident.'*

I could not help, but wonder if the two deaths were related.

Maybe the past caught up with papa after all. Now, I will never know nor have answers to what really happened in his past. Papa is gone and he has taken everything with him, were my only thoughts.

25

First News of My Sister, after 50 Years

The glare from the morning sunshine crept through the lace openings of the curtains, like spiders trying to make their way through a tangled web. I could feel zigzag forms on my face from the sun peering through the curtains. I squinted trying to keep the glare out of my eyes, but it did not help. I crossed my arms over my head and rolled onto my stomach.

Five more minutes, I said to myself as I stretched my arms out with a loud yawn escaping from my mouth.

After a few more minutes of tossing and turning, I slowly made my way out of bed and to the kitchen to prepare a cup of coffee. I put some bread into the toaster and went to the front door to pick up the morning newspaper. I opened the door to see the mailman in the distance.

For once, he is early, I thought and closed the door.

The neighbor's barking dog indicated the postman had arrived. I hurriedly finished the last bits of toast and gulped down the remaining coffee before going out to retrieve the mail. My hand stretched into the mailbox to pull out the normal stack of newsletters and bills. Scrutinizing the mail I muttered, "junk, junk," as I tossed one stack to the side.

As I stooped down to gather the pile of junk that had accumulated, I noticed a worn envelope protruding from the stack. I pulled it out. The envelope was slightly torn, and had several writings on it. A foreign stamp in the upper right corner was visible. It appeared to have been misdirected. It could not be for me. I examined it further. The letter was initially sent to my old address and had been forwarded to my current one. The return address was in written in Cyrillic, however something more interesting appeared. Across the envelope written in English was a bold plea;

PLEASE HELP ME FIND MY LOST RELATIVES.

Who would be sending me such a letter? Surely, it was not good news. I didn't know what to expect as I slowly and carefully opened the envelope. The correspondence was written in Russian. Lucky, I was still able to read and write Russian from my many years of studies at home with papa and from the Russian camps that I attended during the summers.

I gasped as I realized what I was holding in my hand. The letter was from my lost sibling. The older sister who I learned existed fifty years ago and who I unsuccessfully tried to find, had surfaced. She wrote she was living in Baku, Azerbaijan and searching for her American family. I was astonished. I tried so hard to locate my sister and now a half a century later, she had practically arrived at my doorstep.

My sister wrote that Azerbaijan, a former Soviet Republic had become independent, thus giving her the freedom to correspond as she had always wanted, but was unable to because of the previous political situation. Azerbaijan had gained its independence in 1991. Gone were the restrictions and fears of any reprisals from a communist government. The doors of democracy had been opened, giving her the freedom to contact her younger sibling in America, and now allowing us to correspond. Letters began immediately between us, the two Ella's. Through the exchange of letters, I learned more of the life papa left behind in Baku, the day he vanished in 1942. My sister wrote:

"One day, he just disappeared. No one knew what happened to him. He was just gone. There were all kinds of rumors such as the communists had caught up with him and he had suffered the same consequence as his father or the Germans had taken him, but he had escaped. The last we heard was that he was dead. Shortly after his disappearance, Grandmother Maria Kolasova, his mother, also vanished in the middle of the night—an old lady gone, forever, never to be seen or heard from again. There were rumors about her too, that she had been taken to Siberia. We thought they were both dead. Many years passed and then a letter arrived. It was from America, from father. Mama fainted when she received the letter. She cried and cried for days. Everyone thought he was dead, but on the contrary, he was alive. It was quite a shock. He wrote he was living in Connecticut and that he had a new family. He wrote about you. He said he had a daughter that he named after me, Ella Borisovna. I knew about you my entire life. I tried to contact you various ways, but the KGB was always about. I was afraid for myself and my son."

My sister's letter caused me to miss papa more than ever. He could have never imaged that his two daughters would find each other. I told my sister of his demise 17 years ago. How we both wished he was still alive and the three of us were together.

We dreamed of the day we would meet. A reunion to usher in the millennium year of 2000 was arranged. My sister was invited to visit me in Los Angeles.

"Papa could never image that one day we would meet. Could it truly be possible? It seems like a dream that we even found each other," I wrote to my sister in Baku. We counted the days when my newly found sibling would arrive in America. Unexpectedly, a telephone call changed all that was planned.

"How can that be? How could they deny a United States visitor's visa for you? Did you tell them of our circumstances, our story?" I asked as my sister sobbed on the other end of the telephone line.

"I told them everything, but they refused to listen. The interviewer at the consulate was a young America man. He asked me why I wanted to go to America and what I was going to do there. I told him I wanted be united with my sister. He said I don't have any family in Baku to ensure my return, that I had no social standing; therefore, I could not be given a visitor's visa. He is just a young lad; he knows nothing of life. He showed no compassion. We will never see each other," my sister cried further.

I could not believe what I had just heard. It couldn't be possible. Surely, there was a mistake in the translation and the American Embassy in Baku had made an error. I would place a long distance call and speak to them personally. I would explain the facts and would guarantee my sister's return to Baku. Surely, they wouldn't refuse a visa after I explained the situation. I dialed the number to the American Consulate.

"American Consulate, Baku," answered the receptionist.

"I am calling from Los Angeles regarding a visitor's visa for my sister. My sister doesn't speak English and I thought perhaps there was some misunderstanding regarding her application for a visitor's visa," I said.

"Yes, your sister did apply for a visa. It was denied," was the reply.

"No, no, it can't be. There isn't any logically reason why it should be denied. She has round trip ticket. Is there anyone else I can speak to?" I inquired.

"Not at the moment, however, I will pass your concern to our Deputy Chief of Mission."

The next day, I received a fax from the Deputy Chief of Mission in Baku stating, "Ms. Kantemir admitted during the visa interview that she had no remaining relatives in Azerbaijan. She is a pensioner, so it is understandable she does not work; however, she admitted that she has no savings or income from any other source either. When asked about her travel plans, Ms. Kantemir said that she wanted to go to California, but was unclear on what she would do there or how long she would stay. She was unable to give a return date at all. Unfortunately, Ms. Kantemir does not have sufficient ties, economic or social, to be eligible for a non-immigrate visa." It was signed "Elizabeth Sheldon."

My heart dropped. 'Maybe, my sister is right. We will never meet. There is nothing that can be done. We are nothing. We do not have influence to persuade the embassy to reconsider on the grounds of humanitarian reasons. Endless years of waiting mattered to no one. Have we found one another to never meet? There must be a way, I thought.

I placed another disappointing call to my sister in Baku.

"Don't lose hope. We have found each other and that is most important. One day, I don't know how, I don't know when, but we will meet. That is a promise. You must believe that," was the only consolation I could give my weeping sister. Sadness, tears and shattered dreams ushered in the new millennium of 2000.

26

Meeting My Sister, a Half Century Later

Three years of writing letters to various government agencies, senators and even President Clinton, pleading for assistance, went in vain. Our pleas were ignored. No one was able or interested to help. There seemed to be no solution for a reunification between us. There was only one way I would ever meet my sister. I had made up my mind!

I will travel to Azerbaijan, I thought.

Amidst warnings of *"It's too dangerous, the people and country are in turmoil. It's not safe anywhere!"* did not deter me. I was compelled to make the journey. Nothing could hold me from meeting my long lost sister. I had promised her years earlier, we would meet. I would keep that promise and make the long trip to Azerbaijan. I looked at the photograph of my sister that papa had carried his entire life in his left shirt pocket close to his heart. It was mine now. I put it in my passport. It would be there for our first meeting.

The flight from Los Angeles to London's Heathrow Airport was ten hours. The next flight from Heathrow to Baku would be another five hours. My heart beat faster with the anticipation of meeting my sister. Papa could have never imaged that the two of us would ever meet, or could he have? He was a perceptive man and probably even expected this outcome had he lived longer. An announcement made by the captain interrupted my thoughts.

"Due to aircraft congestion we will need to circle for an additional 30 minutes before we are allowed to land at Heathrow."

I looked at my watch. I would have to hurry when the plane landed. I would not have much time to make my connecting flight to Baku. Nervously, I kept looking out the airplane window. When the plane finally touched down and began its taxi to the terminal I was relieved, but it was only short-lived as another announcement was made.

"Ladies and Gentleman, I am sorry to inform you there is no gate available for us at the moment. We will have to wait on the ramp for another 20 minutes until one opens up and we can taxi to the terminal."

I tensed up and I could feel my heart pounding. There was a possibility that I might miss my connecting plane for now there was only the bare minimum time between the two flights. I began to sweat nervously as I checked my watch again. Unconsciously, my fingers tapped the edge of the armrest. I was anxious, dreading that I would not be able to make my next flight. At last, the aircraft began its slow approach to the terminal and to the gate. When the aircraft door opened, I pushed pass the crowd and ran to the tube that would take me to Heathrow's Terminal Five. I just had to make the flight. Another 5 hours and I would be reunited with my sister.

Arriving at Terminal Five, I continued to run to the airline counter.

"You are late. We have accepted standbys and the flight is closed," said the agent when I arrived.

"No, no. My plane was held up fifty minutes on the taxiway. Please. My sister is expecting me in Baku," I pleaded.

"Sorry, Madame, it is no use. The plane is full and there are no seats available," was the reply.

"Are you sure?" I asked.

"Yes, but let me check the computer once more. Yes, it is full. The boarding process is just about completed."

The news was disheartening. This was just another delay in meeting my sister, but I had no choice, but to accept the fact. What was one day after all the decades of waiting.

"Can you send a message to my sister in Baku and let her know I will be delayed one day? Here is her number," I pressed further without giving her a chance to reply negatively. As I handed the note with the information to the clerk, the counter telephone rang.

"What? Okay. I have one customer here. I will send her to the gate," answered the clerk. "Hurry, miss, there is one passenger that did not show up at the gate. You can have the seat, but you must run."

What a twist of fate! I could not believe what I had just heard. The only explanation was that papa was watching over me. I dashed to the gate, barely making it in time. As I collapsed into my seat, the aircraft door closed behind me. I was exhausted. My mind was rampant with thoughts of what to expect not only from my sister, but from a remote country, Azerbaijan. I knew that the summer of 2003 in my sister's country was going to be memorable.

The Republic of Azerbaijan, crossroads of Eastern Europe and Western Asia is a nation with a majority Muslim population. Independent from the Soviet Union since 1991, it is surrounded by Iran on the south, Armenia on the west, Russian to the north, and Turkey to the northwest. The Baku-Tbilisi-Ceyhan pipeline transports oil from the Caspian Sea to international markets. I had heard much about the beauty of Baku from papa, of its wealth of historical and ancient heritage, and of papa's desire to one day return. His spoken words of the country where he once lived echoed in my head as the plane landed in Baku. The flight between Los Angeles and Baku was nearly 24 hours door-to-door. I felt very safe when I arrived. Fortunately, it turned out that those warnings I heard weren't true at all; the country wasn't anything like people had described.

I was surprised how easy it was to get a visa at the airport and how friendly the airport immigration officers were. That impression of warmth and hospitality remained the entire visit in Azerbaijan. As soon as I passed through customs and collected my luggage, I started looking for my sister. Although, the age old worn photo of a young blonde toddler in my hand was the only clue that would bring us together, I felt I would recognize my sister instantly. I looked at the photo and then at the crowd in front of me. How would I ever find my sister! She had to be there! Out of nowhere, a petite Tatar looking woman with a big charming smile appeared from among the crowd. She took a step forward and I knew instantly that it was my sister. It seemed a fairy tale come true and "*all that we see or seem is but a dream within a dream,*" (Edgar Allan Poe) came to my mind.

"Ella," said my sister as she stretched her arms out towards me.

Tears rolled down my face as I walked towards my sister. Words were not needed to describe the feeling between us as

we embraced. Tears of happiness streamed down our faces—
the two *Ella Kantemirs!* I noticed that other people in the crowd
were crying, too. It turns out that they were my sister's dearest
friends and their families. They had come to welcome me.

What wonderful people, these people of Baku. My sister
and I walked happily, arm in arm, feeling complete, now that
we had found one another. We got into waiting cars for the
drive into the city. Since my sister didn't speak English, we
spoke in Russian, which I had not forgotten from my childhood. We arrived at Abbasova Road where my sister lived and
we climbed the four flights of stairs to her apartment; followed
by friends who carried my heavy suitcases a top their heads.

I entered the small two-room apartment. A table was set up
with food and drinks. Russian and Azerbaijani music filled the
room and everyone began to dance. Everyone treated me as a
close friend and family member. I was encouraged to try ethic
foods and learn the local folk dance. Everyone asked many
questions about America for they have never met anyone from
the United States. I in turn, wanted to learn about Azerbaijan.

The celebration continued into the early morning hours and
until we were all were exhausted. My sister and I discovered
we were alike in thought and manner. It was as if we were
never separated and had spent our entire lives together.

I could not wait to explore the city that papa spoke so fondly
of. I desperately wanted to see "Old Baku" and stroll along the
boulevard with its many parks.

The 'Qara Qarayev' metro station would take us to old Baku.
We took the long escalator down into the metro that was decorated in gray marble and had artwork representing Azerbaijan.
A gush of air from the tunnel indicated the train was in route
and would arrive shortly. It quickly filled with passengers. I
was impressed when I saw young men eagerly give up their
seats for the elderly, women with children, and ladies of all ages.

I noticed that each spotless metro station we passed had exquisite works of Azerbaijan culture. They seemed more a museum than a metro stop. It was evident the country was proud of its heritage and traditions that were displayed in the care of their metros. Arriving at our destination, we took another long escalator with dozens of lighted lamps along the handrail and up to the top of the station. We were in *Icheri Sheher*, the walled inner city of Baku. As my sister and I walked arm in arm as was the custom, I could imagine Baku in the 15th century when the Silk Road was the popular trade route. I could envision vendors in the streets, haggling and selling carpets, crafts, and clothing in the stalls of the many narrow cobbled-stoned streets, as the vendors were now doing now.

Maiden's Tower caught my eye. It was the landmark of old Baku, built in the 12th century on the shore of the Caspian Sea. Due to the recession of the waters, now the tower stood on a busy main street surrounded by gardens. Legend has it that a maiden threw herself off the top into the sea below when she was not allowed to marry her lover. A climb to the top of the Maiden tower displayed a panoramic view of Baku, its old fortress walls, and the beautiful Caspian Sea. Many freighter ships and oil drill platforms were visible in the distance. I breathed in the sea air, enjoying the picturesque view of the city of Baku and its spectacular coastline.

"Look over there. In 1930 that once housed a gastronome center noted for delicious Russian *pirog* (fried dough, filled with minced meat or mashed potato). That's where our father used to buy *pirog*. Mother worked there and sold him the best *pirogi* in the city. That is where they met," said my sister.

I could imagine the hustle and bustle of the 1930's gastronome. It was hard to believe I was actually looking at the building that papa once frequented. We made our way down the winding staircase of the tower and into the maze of alleys, passing caravansaries *(ancient inns)* that had been refurbished into modern restaurants, and to the *Palace of the Shirvanshah.* The palace was the seat of the ruling dynasty during the Middle Ages, constructed in 1411. The complex contained the Shah's mosque with minarets on each side of its corners. The mosque had two chapels for prayers, a large one for men and a smaller area for women. Housed within, were burial vaults and almost modern mausoleums.

The famous Boulevard with its many water fountains was the next stop. Each fountain was more beautiful than the one before. In the evening the fountains lit up with colors of yellow and turquoise. We continued our walk along the Boulevard until we reached the shores of the Caspian Sea. Many outdoor cafes lined the shoreline. Taking a rest, we sat at an outdoor cafe, ordered tea and watched the people, dressed in their finest garments stroll under the moonlit skies by the sea. It was a pleasure to see happy couples, young and old, holding hands, and children running about as they enjoyed their treat of ice-cream.

The following day intense heat engulfed the city. My sister and I cooled ourselves by swimming at one of the many beaches near the Caspian Sea where I gathered seashells for my daughters back home on the opposite end of the earth.

We were invited to the homes of my sister's many friends, to dine, dance and exchange cultural thoughts. I was quickly accepted as one of their own. I was introduced to what for me again was exotic food and music. My favorite food became *gutab, rice pilaf, kebab* and of course, Azerbaijani beer. Once dinner was concluded, dancing followed.

I was introduced to the charming movements of one of Azerbaijani many folk dances, *Ceyran bala,* an old dance with elegant movements. I even attempted the fast tempo of the men's dance 'Zorkhana,' with its high energy signifying brav-ery and courage. By the end of my stay I even began to learn some Azerbaijan words. In those three short weeks I grew to love the culture and people of Baku. But, most importantly, we were able to celebrate my sister's 65th birthday together!

We discovered so many ways in which we're alike. We both look like our father and our voices are quite similar to each other. We even think alike and share similar tastes. Papa, who died in 1982 in the U.S., had wanted so much to go back to Baku. Finally, after so many years I managed to go in his place. That visit bought me closer and more than I could ever have imagined to papa, and now I understood why he loved Azerbai-jan so much. Now, I considered it my country and people too.

And that photo, papa used to carry in his shirt pocket? Well, both my sister and I have a copy of it. Our big wish is for my sister to get a chance to visit the United States. If that happens, we want to go together to visit the grave of our father—whose longing for Baku brought us together. The sister that I learned about so long ago in the backyard of a small Connecticut town in 1953 became a reality in 2003—a fifty year span!

One would think the story ended there, with a happy end-ing. However, the unexplained events continued to occur. A pending trip to Russian with the story of my sister's reunion would bring about a surprise and unexpected revelation; con-firmation of a KGB's secret police hunt for papa.

27

Anya and the KGB — Russia, 2004

The reunion between my sister and myself caused me to reminisce of my cousin Anya, who in 1971 had visited the United States. At that time, the communist government allowed Anya to leave the Soviet Union and visit my family in America. Her husband was not approved to leave the Soviet Union, so Anya made the trip without him. I have not seen Anya since the 1971 visit and was anxious to reconnect with her. Feeling confident since I was able to arrange an almost impossible reunion with my sister, I decided visiting Anya would be an easier feat. The policies of the Soviet Union had changed, for it was now a Russian democratic government. It would be an entirely different scenario from my Soviet tour of 1967. With this in mind, I departed for Russia.

Anya and her family were waiting for me when I arrived

at Rostov International Airport in southern Russia. She was standing at the customs exit, her arms full of flowers with other family members alongside. I recognized Anya immediately. She had not changed through all the years.

"Anya, how wonderful to see you, after all this time, you look exactly the same, not a bit different," I exclaimed as she approached me. She handed me the bouquet of flowers as everyone gathered around to exchange hugs and kisses. My two suitcases loaded with gifts were put into the trunk of a dirty old car. With all formalities set aside we all climbed in for the trip to Anya's home.

Anya's residence was a four-story apartment complex that was built during the Soviet era. There was no elevator in the building and everyone had to make their way up the stairs. Anya's apartment was decorated in traditional Russian style. Colorful rugs hung on the walls and handmade white doilies lined the sofas. A samovar sat on top of the buffet that was filled with crystal glasses and fine tableware. In the center of the living room was a long table with rows of chairs. The table was covered with assorted appetizers prepared from homegrown vegetables, alongside bottles of wine and vodka. Rows of fresh tomatoes, cucumbers and eggplant lined the table. Homemade vodka, humorously called *Channel Number Three* flowed freely into the night and morning hours. It was served again with breakfast as vodka was a Russian institution and a perquisite during meals.

The following day, I toured the cellar in the building where Anya lived. The cold dirt underground room housed several layers of shelves that contained produce and canned goods of various sorts. Vegetables and fruits were preserved for the winter months when fresh food was scare. Fresh squeezed tomato juice in glass containers along the shelves was visible. The huge display of canned stored goods prompted me to blurt out, "Anya, you are the Martha Stewart of Russia."

"This is what we must do each year, before the cold weather sets in. Everything is grown and canned at the end of summer to prepare for the winter months ahead. Sacks full of potatoes are kept here. It is cold enough and refrigeration is not needed. The produce is sufficient until summer arrives and we start all over with the same process," said Anya.

"I must sample your home made tomato juice," I said.

"Very well, let's go upstairs. I have a bottle of juice there," replied Anya.

I settled in the kitchen as Anya proudly poured me a glass of homemade tomato juice.

"Anya, I was in Azerbaijan last year. I have a sister there and after decades I was finally able to meet her. I wrote an article about our meeting that I would like to share with you."

I took the *Azerbaijan International*, Autumn 2003, magazine issue that I had brought along and opened to page 11, "Sisters Meet — Half a Century Later."

"My sister and I have the same father, Boris Ivanovich Kantemir and we also share the same name," I continued.

Anya's mouth fell wide open as she placed her hand to her mouth.

"Anya, are you that surprised that I have a sister in Baku and that we share the same name?" I asked, a bit confused not expecting such a dramatic reaction.

"Kantemir? Did you say Kantemir? " asked Anya.

"Yes, what is so astonishing about that? My sister carries our father's name, Kantemir," I replied.

"I am not surprised that you have found a long lost sister. It is Uncle Boris's name that surprises me. I had no idea it was Kantemir and as a result, when I was questioned by the KGB upon my return from visiting your family in 1971, I denied knowing such a person," exclaimed Anya.

"Anya, what are you talking about?" I was baffled. My

cousin's revelation confirmed all previous suspicions of Soviet operatives that have haunted our family for years.

Anya continued with her story. "Circumstances prevented me from telling you what happened when I returned home to the Soviet Union from my visit in 1971, but I will tell you now. I received a call from the *Committee for State Security,* our secret police organization known as the KGB. I was told to report to their offices for questioning. Once I arrived, I was escorted through a long corridor with many doors on each side. I went through one of those doors into a room that looked like a cell. A small cluster of tables with electronic equipment and earphones were set up. A muscular man approached me and I knew it could be nothing good. He introduced himself as the chairman of the *Seventh Directorate,* a Mr. Yuri Andropov. I knew that to be the KGB and I was puzzled as to why the KGB was interested in me. Have I been accused of anti-Communists activities during my trip to the U.S.? To my knowledge I haven't done anything against our government.

"Mr. Andropov looked down at my feet and then slowly followed every curve of my body to the top of my head. It gave me the creeps and caused the hair on my arms to stand up. It was as if I was being electrocuted. He told me in a stern tone that I have been under surveillance for a long time and that they had many questions to ask of me. I began to shake, for I knew I was in some kind of trouble. I stood there, like a dog with its tail between its legs and told him I have done nothing illegal in the Soviet Union. He said he was not interested in me, that he was only interested in my recent trip to America to visit relatives, and specifically Boris Ivanovich Kantemir. He asked me if I saw such a person.

"Of course I told him I did not know this person that he is inquiring about. He asked me several more times about a Boris Ivanovich Kantemir. I told him I don't know anyone by that name. He did not believe me and said that they knew where I went and what I did and that I did have contact with this person. They threatened to keep me there all day if I did not confess that I knew a Boris Kantemir. I told Mr. Andropov that I only visited my uncle Boris Karanwytsch, and repeated that I did not know the person they were seeking. I was told to stand in that room until my memory returned. I stood there alone for a few hours. The secret police thought I was hiding something, but eventually realized I was naive and knew nothing.

"I overheard them say that they were confident that I had no information on Kantemir and his activities. They said he was witty and they believed he used the name Ali-khan when he fled the Caucasus, but they were not sure. It must have been his writings as an editor of the publication, 'Caucasus' in Germany because he wrote memorandums examining the *Caucasus question*' and recruited followers who founded the *Northern Caucasus National Committee* in 1941. He engaged Soviet prisoners of war from the Northern Caucasus and persuaded them to enroll in the military formations of the German Reich. They also said that it was his revenge against our Communist State for confiscating his family's properties in their efforts to make the Soviet people all equal. They tracked Kantemir to Connecticut and even one of his supporters, Nicholas, unwittingly gave them his location before they took care of him permanently. They concluded that they had taken care of Nicholas and Boris would be next.

"I stood for one hour in that tiny room, all alone and not knowing what to think. I had no information to give them, as I did not know such a person. They asked me many questions and I didn't know what they were talking about and I didn't know what they were searching for. They were not satisfied with my response and I had to return several times to their offices. They asked many questions about Boris Ivanovich

Kantemir and Uncle Boris. I only knew Uncle Boris. They finally released me, saying I could not be of any assistance to them and that I was oblivious to their politics. They said I was not needed any longer and they would do what needed to be done without elaborating further. I was totally confused by the entire scenario.

"I didn't understand it at the time, but I understand now why the KGB was so interested in Uncle Boris. The story of your search for your sister made me realize that Uncle Boris and the person they were seeking are actually the one and the same. They sensed I didn't have any knowledge and eventually, they stopped calling me to their offices. I don't know. Did the KGB ever find Uncle Boris?"

"Anya," I said, "the KGB knew what you didn't at the time. It was not a coincidence that you were permitted to leave the Soviet Union in 1971 to visit our family and your husband was denied. You were used. You were the bait! The Soviets wanted information on my father and the KGB was closing in on what was a closely guarded secret. They found father's friend in New Jersey. He was murdered. No wonder papa was always looking over his shoulder. He knew! The KGB was not able to get concrete evidence when they interrogated you. That explains the puzzling and mysterious behavior of papa. He was afraid the KGB would eventually find him. He did not know that they were right on his trail. Now, thirty three years later, I learn they, in fact, had found him. If I did not have the reunion with my sister, if I had not shown you the published story of *Sisters Meet — Half a Century Later* in Azerbaijan International Magazine, we would have never known the truth and have confirmation of all that was suspected in the past."

"Ella, I remember when visiting Uncle Boris in Connecticut, he told me that during his time in Cherkessk he buried a valuable bag containing riches near a fence and close to a tree.

This bag was given to him by his grandfather, Gregory who inherited from his grandfather," said Anya.

"Yes, we all have heard that story," I replied. "The ancient bag is lost in time. It would be a miracle if it was ever found. Unfortunately, they remain undiscovered to this day."

It was then that I remembered the circumstance of papa's death; an unexplained heart attack on the operating table. Did the KGB have anything to do with it? That unsettling thought would continue to haunt me my entire life.

28

Searching for the Dmitri Kantemir's Estate and Heirlooms

Los Angeles, California, 2005. It was a chaotic day at one of the nation's busiest airports. The unusual weather at Los Angeles International Airport had played havoc leaving thousands of passengers stranded. Finally the heavy downpour of rain let up and soon things got back to normal. I worked at my computer, in the back office, of one of the major airlines and had successfully re-booked almost all the affected passengers on later flights. My back ached and I was exhausted from dealing with difficult travelers. Sipping on a cup of vanilla latte, my concentration was interrupted when I heard Pat, my co-worker asked me.

"Ella, guess where I am going on my vacation?"

I looked up from my computer and stretched my body trying to straighten up my back.

"Well, wherever you go, make sure you don't travel in the rainy season. You don't want to experience anything like today," I said.

"No worry about the weather where we are going. It's going to be the best time of the year to travel to Istanbul, Turkey. Not only that, Ron and I know a wonderful guide who is from Turkey and knows everything there is about the country," said Pat.

That got my interest and my eyes widened with excitement. I had always wanted to visit Turkey, but more so, I wanted to learn more of a country that was not only rich in culture and once the center of civilization, but a country that might dwell more insight into the life and times of my ancestor, Prince Dmitri Kantemir who was exiled there in his early years.

Turkey, a country situated on two continents had a long intriguing history. Istanbul served as a capital city not only of the Roman Empire in (330-395), the Byzantine Empire in (395-1204 and 1261-1453), the Latin Empire (1204-1261) and the one I had the most interest in, the Ottoman Empire (1453-1922).

Constantinople, now Istanbul was made capital of the Ottoman Empire in 1453 by Sultan Mehmed II, the *Conqueror* after a 53-day siege. It was Sultan Mehmed who created the Grand Bazaar and rejuvenated the city religiously by inviting fleeing Orthodox and Catholic inhabitants to return. By doing this he wanted to form a diverse and unique cosmopolitan society. Several architectural monuments were also constructed, including the Topkapi Palace and the Eyup Sultan Mosque.

Constantine the Great had built Istanbul, a fabled trade and religious center, known as 'The City on Seven Hills.' The metropolis in 324, matched the Seven Hills of Rome, but with a mosque capping each hill. They overlook the southern Bosporus strait and a natural harbor known as the Golden Horn, placing the city on two continents—the western portion in Europe and the eastern portion in Asia.

I was hoping to learn more about my ancestors through Turkey's history. I felt the country was a contributing source to the foundation of Dmitri's extensive knowledge. Turkey was and still is a country that astonishes and captivates its visitors. Surely evidence still existed of the valuable contributions made by the great Dmitri Kantemiroglu. (Turkish version of surname) I would ask Pat for her help to locate any remnants of his past.

"Pat would you and Ron do me a favor while in Istanbul? Would it be possible for you to try to locate where my ancestor lived? He was well known in his time and there may be still some relics left of his past."

"Really, I'll ask our guide who lives in Turkey. If anyone can find anything of your ancestor it would be Ferit. He is a walking encyclopedia and knows Turkey inside out. He is also our friend and knows we are coming," said Pat.

"Great! I don't expect too much since it was so long ago, but any findings would be most helpful. Let me jot down what I know and it will be a start," I said.

I reached for a sheet of paper and began to write.

"DMITRI KANTEMIR LIVED IN ISTANBUL FROM 1688 UNTIL 1710.

IN TURKEY HE WAS KNOWN AS DMITRI KANTERMIROGLU."

I wondered if that small bit of information would be enough to bring any results. I wanted to learn more about the ancestors that papa spoke about and of a time that once was. I sat there in deep thought.

"Hey, Ella, wake-up," I have asked you twice already. Do you want us to locate your ancestor or not?" questioned Pat.

"Oh, yes of course," I replied and handed over the notepaper:

Searching for the Dmitri Kantemir's Estate and Heirlooms | 249

Istanbul, Turkey, 2005: 'If one had but a simple glance to give the world, one should gaze on Istanbul's—Alphonse le Lamartine . . .

Rain pelted the airplane window. The Turkish airliner was on its final approach into Ataturk Airport. Pat looked out the window trying to get any glimpse of Istanbul from the air; however, heavy raindrops obscured most of her vision.

"I cannot believe it's raining; it must have followed us from Los Angeles," she said.

"Move a little, let me see if I can make anything out," answered Ron.

He looked out the window, straining to see if he could recognize anything that he had read about from his guide books. Through the clouds, he could vaguely make out the Bosporus strait. The body of water formed the boundary between the European and Asian part of Turkey. The Bosporus was the narrowest passage between the Black Sea and the Mediterranean Sea. Being of significance, it was one of the deciding factors of Roman Emperor, Constantine the Great to form his new capital. Constantinople was the capital of the Eastern Roman Empire. Later, when the Ottoman Turks seized power, it was renamed Istanbul.

Stretching her neck further, Pat saw a body of water similar to the shape of a horn.

"Oh, that must be the Golden Horn, an inlet of the Bosporus that divides the city of Istanbul and forms a natural harbor," said Pat as she reached into her bag for her guidebook of Turkey.

"Here is the page with information on the Golden Horn. It says, according to Greek legend, the name Golden Horn is derived from *Keroessa*, the mother of *Byzas the Megarian*, who named it after her, the Greek name being *Chryson Keras*.

In Turkish it is called *Haliç*, pronounced Hah-Leech, which means a body of water that separates the old and new. The deep natural harbor encloses with the Sea of Marmara. It used to be the naval headquarters for the Byzantine Empire and its walls were built along the shoreline to protect the city of Constantinople from naval attacks. A large chain was pulled across from Constantinople to the old town of Galata at the entrance to prevent unwanted ships from entering."

As Pat finished reading the article, the plane touched down with a slight thud and began its taxi to the terminal. As if on cue, the rain stopped. Rays of sunshine peaked out from behind the white billowy clouds and lit up the skies.

"Amazing! Istanbul is the heart of civilization," stated Pat.

The plane taxied until it reached the terminal building. Once the aircraft door opened, the couple scrambled to the immigration area. Luckily, it was not crowded as they were in a hurry not to keep Ferit waiting. They proceeded to collect their bags and excitedly exited the terminal.

"There's Ferit!" exclaimed Ron.

"Hello and welcome to Istanbul," said Ferit, as he hugged both Pat and Ron.

"It is nice to see you on this side of the world and now I will drive you to your hotel for a day's rest before we get started tomorrow. We will get started early to explore old Istanbul. It will be there we will most likely find anything of your friend's ancestor that you wrote to me about. The tour will give you a first-hand experience of this unique city. A city built on two continents. It embraces both Western and Asian cultures and it was the capital of three magnificent empires. Istanbul had many names throughout its course of history. It was known as the *Great City*, the *City of Emperors*, and the *City of Seven Hills*. Each hill was represented with a mosque. You will see a city of inspiration. There are mosques, churches, synagogues, and Istanbul's combination of religions makes me feel it is the soul of civilization. Well, here we are. Let's get into the car and I will explain some sights to you on our way to your hotel. Come now, let's put these suitcases in the back and get started. I promise, tomorrow I will drive even slower as I don't want you to miss any beauty of our exotic city," he said.

Ron climbed in the front seat next to Ferit and Pat made herself comfortable in the back. Even though dusk was soon approaching, the sun was still shinning wrapping the city in its golden glow. As the entourage drove along the many narrow roads they tried to take in all the highlights along the way. It seemed as if they were in caught in another era of time.

"Look! There it is! The Basilica of Saint Sophia. Justinian the Great built it in the 6th century. Originally, it was a basilica, later a mosque, but now it's a museum. It is one of the most beautiful buildings in the world and the epitome of Byzantine architecture. Many holy relics are housed there including a 50 foot silver iconostasis. The Basilica of Saint Sophia was once the religious center of the Orthodox Byzantine Empire for 1000 years and the patriarchal church of the Patriarch of Constantinople.

After the Ottoman Turks conquered it in 1453 Sultan Mehmed II converted it into a mosque and they removed the altar and all the iconostasis. Over the course of time Islamic features were added, such as the four minarets. Saint Sophia served as a model for many Ottoman mosques. Contrary to the name, it remained a mosque until 1935 when it was converted into a museum by the Republic of Turkey. Saint Sophia is dedicated to the Holy Wisdom of God rather than a specific saint named Sophia," said Ferit.

Just then, out of nowhere, a dazzling sight appeared, both

Ron and Pat cold not take their eyes off the structure that was now basking in the sunset.

"That is the Topkapi Palace. It has that affect all everyone. It was the home to all the Ottoman sultans. It dates back to 1453. Sultan Mehmed the Conqueror, used the most expensive and rare materials in the layout of the palace. You are looking at its main portal, named *Bab-I Humayun*. The palace consists of four courts and various structures and up to 4,000 people resided in it at one time, including janissaries, the Imperial Council, Grand Vizers and of course, the Harem. The Harem was home to the Sultan's mother, concubines and wives of the Sultan. It also included his children and servants and up to 300 women, children and eunuchs were housed and then there were many courtyards, chambers, passages, halls and pavilions full with Ottoman treasures and jewelry. One can really see the wonder of Ottoman style in the architecture. It is now a museum and parts of it are opened to the public," said Ferit.

A faint melody of Ottoman music interrupted the tranquility of the evening and prevented Ferit from continuing his oration. Spellbound they listened to the music until it faded from their ears, but not from their memory.

"What was that haunting music?" asked Ron.

"That was the 'Table Clock' from within the Topkapi Museum. The clock was manufactured at the beginning of the 18th century. It plays eight musical pieces a day composed by our early Turkish musicians who developed our Ottoman music," replied Ferit.

"Certainly enchanting music," replied Pat.

Ron turned his head to take a look as the car passed the Topkapi Palace. The sight hypnotized him. He didn't take his eyes off the white Imperial gate until it was out of sight and then for a moment and only a moment, he thought he saw a glow in its place, a glow emulating the brilliance of a massive yellow diamond. Ron's hypnotic state was only broken when he heard Ferit say.

"We have arrived at your hotel. Let's put your bags into your room. We still have time for Turkish coffee, before you retire. The coffee house next door is noted for our traditional coffee. You must have a taste of it on your first night here."

They crammed into the small elevator that would take them to the upper floors of the hotel. It was the only modern piece of technology in the place. A slight aroma of incense welcomed them as they stepped out onto the second level. Gold lamps lined the walls of the dimly lit hallway, but the bold colors of red and gold floor carpeting guided them on.

"Here is your room. Just put your things in and we shall go," said Ferit as they made their way through the wooden arched doorway.

Pat and Ron set their bags down and glanced about the room. It was quaint and had a double bed with overstuffed gold leafed pillows that accentuated the red satin bed coverings.

"Reminds me of Ali Baba and the forty thieves," said Pat.

An open window displayed an exotic view of nighttime Istanbul. The backdrop of a dark Turkish night was enhanced by the silhouette of a crescent moon. In the distance, bluish white lights illuminated a spectacular mosque.

"That is the *Blue Mosque*. It was built between 1609 and 1616, during the rule of Ahmed I. It is called the Blue Mosque for the blue tiles covering the walls of the interior. It is made out of stone and marble. There are six minarets, four of which stand at the corners of the mosque and the other two at the end of the forecourt. At sunset one is able to hear the evening prayers. Enough said, let's end the evening with our famous Turkish coffee," continued Ferit.

Ron and Pat settled in their chairs at the coffee house. They enjoyed listening to Ferit with his stories of Turkey and its amazing culture.

"Coffee was brought to Istanbul by Syrian traders in 1555. Turkish coffee played an important role in the Turkish lifestyle from the Ottoman Empire to the present. In the 17th century it was part of elaborate ceremonies in the Ottoman court. Women in the harem received intensive training in the technique of preparing proper coffee. A woman's merit was based on the taste of her coffee. Even now, coffee is the center of interaction. Men and women socialize over coffee, at home, in cafes, and in coffee houses. Coffee itself, is a means to meet and talk. Our coffee is derived from the Arabic bean. At times, cardamom, a spice, is added to give an aromatic taste. When one is finished drinking, the cup is turned upside down on the saucer and allowed to cool. A fortune reading from the left over grinds is performed."

"This coffee is wonderful and so are your very informative and beautiful stories," said Pat, as she finished the last drop.

"We are not finished yet. Turn your cup over and I will read your fortune from the grinds, as I have been taught," replied Ferit.

When in Rome, do as the Romans, and when in Turkey, do as the Turkish, thought Pat as she turned her cup over.

Ferit studied the few remaining grinds with amusement, and said, "Ah, I see your fortune very clearly. There is a Turkish saying, *to drink a cup of coffee together guarantees forty years of friendship.* That is your fortune. Our friendship will last forty years and more, and our friendship will continue tomorrow when I take you on a journey back in time—an endless voyage with discovering the treasures of Istanbul in the magnificent country of Turkey. As Napoleon Bonaparte said, *'If the Earth were a single state, Istanbul would be its capital.'*"

As they wandered through the narrow streets of old Istanbul, Pat and Ron did their best to keep up with Ferit who was way ahead for he was eagerly looking forward to finding something new in this old city. He thought he knew everything culturally and historically about Istanbul, but this would be a fresh adventure for him and he knew exactly where to start, to find the house of Dmitri Kantermiroglu. It would be in the old Fener district, the Greek quarter of Constantinople that was once the residence of privileged Greek families. The Fener area was home to most of the Greeks who remained in the city after the fall of Constantinople in 1453.

The Greek residents of Fener were called Phanariotes. Wealthy Phanariotes were appointed rulers of Wallachia and Moldavia (modern day Romania) by the Ottoman Empire. The Phanariotes developed Fener into a cultural and religious center and eventually, the Eastern Orthodox Patriarchate of Constantinople moved to Fener and is still located there to the present day.

Pat and Ron lagging behind Ferit stopped occasionally to admire the country's unusual landscape.

"This must be the most beautiful stretch of scenery in Turkey," said Pat who could not help but notice the historic waterfront houses stretching along the coast of the Bosphorus.

The coast was lined with palaces, gardens and ruins of old Ottoman wooden houses called *Yali*. Equally visible were the Castles of Europe, built on the Bosphorus by the Ottoman Turks to block sea traffic and prevent any support ships of the Byzantine from reaching Constantinople during the Turkish siege of the city in the early 1400's. The castles served as fortifications that were built on each side of the strait.

The party's search took them further along an area of ancient winding cobble stoned streets. Cracked gray stone walls appeared between old apartments. Each apartment had a colorful balcony painted in green, blue, yellow and orange.

Looking up above at the balconies, they noticed clothes hung out to dry, fluttering in the breeze. The group continued on and stopped only when they saw a merchant selling his produce of yellow bananas from a wooden wagon. It reminded them that they were hungry as now it was a few of hours since they first began their search.

"Bananas, bananas," chanted the merchant who was standing by his wagon.

"Let's stop for a moment. I'm famished and am anxious to try some of those bananas," said Pat.

She purchased several bananas. Before she could finish paying for them, Ferit was already on his way, eager to accomplish the mission of the day.

"Wait, wait for me!" yelled Pat running after him holding the plastic bag full of bananas swaying in her hand.

The trio continued on; walking, uphill, downhill, and around a corner. More colored stoned walls of gray, white, brown, and orange appeared. What seemed an endless row of cobbled stoned streets continued on until one cobble stoned street appeared like no other. A sparkling silver glow within a cracked stone sidewalk illuminated the walkway that led them to twenty-two silver cracked stone steps. They followed the steps, climbing up to the end which led them to a towering ancient gray stoned building with arched wooden doors. Gray stoned walls were on each side of the wooden doors as if to protect what was behind the entry and to prohibit anyone from entering the premises. Silver tiles on the stoned walls created a mystic aura. Was it an omen to deter intruders? Pat and Ron could not contain themselves and slowly crept closer and quietly towards the huge wooden doors.

"Woof! Woof!"

With fright, they immediately jumped back at the echoing sound of snarling, barking dogs.

"Get back you miserable creatures," shouted an elderly man from behind the doors.

A key could be heard unlocking the gate. The decrepit doors made a loud creak as they were pushed open by long skinny arms. An old scruffy man appeared from behind the doors with a huge key dangling from his belt. He stared at Ron and Pat and then his eyes shifted to Ferit. He did not know what to think or make of these visitors. No one had come here for many years, and few knew of its existence, except for some inhabitants of the Fener and Balat district.

"I am the guard here, what do you want?" he asked in a grumpy voice.

He was not happy to have his comfortable life turned upside down. He was the care keeper of these historical grounds, caring for them since a young lad. He considered it a privilege and made a promise to watch over the grounds that once were a cultural part of great Istanbul; in the days that once were and never will be again. He did not like these people coming to stir up the dust because all which was, had to rest in peace. He took this personally upon himself for he alone was responsible and would not allow anyone to disturb the tranquility of these beautiful ruins. But now, these strangers had arrived, to probe and intrude, to step foot where they don't belong and were not wanted.

"Sorry to disturb you sir. May we take a look? Our friend's ancestors might have lived here," replied Ron.

"There is nothing to see as most of this place is in ruins and it is very old. It belonged to the Cantacuzenes family, one of the most respected families in the district of Fener. Only a courtyard with a church still exists. The church is dedicated to St. George. According to Orthodox tradition this church was built as the office for the Patriarch of Jerusalem in Istanbul. That is all I can tell you."

"Please, may we look? We won't be long. It's very important. Our friend is a descendant of Prince Dmitri Kantemir. We made a promise to her," said Pat.

The guard almost lost his grip on the leash that the two large watchdogs were attached to. A descendant of the great Dmitri Kantermiroglu whose grounds he had been caring for since childhood? Could it be possible? He would be cursed if he did not let these people in. He was not happy, but he would not stand in the way of fate.

"Don't worry, go take your look. I will put the dogs in their cages until you are finished," moaned the guard.

He stepped aside and allowed the three of them to enter the courtyard. Ancient ruins remained where once stood a great palace. Dilapidated roofs, broken caved in walls exposed what once were majestic rooms and corridors that now are covered with overgrown bush and grass emerging from the wrecked interiors of the palace. Visible and intact, ornate double white doors, majestic with its blue trim, still stood on the upper floors. Centuries passed through those doors. If only they could speak! The church of St. George fared better. It's architect in a form of a basilica structure was still intact, and although, not very ornate, a considerable amount of marble still remained throughout the interior.

"Look here!" exclaimed Pat, when she entered past the wooden doors. "There's something on the stone wall. I can't see it very well. It's covered with overgrown ivy. Let me try to clear it."

Pat pulled the winding plant from the plaque, but the writing was too dirty to decipher. She took a scarf from her head and began to wipe away the soil.

"It has something written on it," she said as she tried to make out the lettering.

A long legged hairy spider quickly darted across the plaque, as if knowing it was in the way.

"Move," said Pat as she brushed the spider aside. "I'm trying to see what is written. Ferit, help! It's in Turkish."

Ferit came running towards Pat. He studied the plaque before reading it out loud:

BU YERDE 1688—1701 TARIHLEKI ARASINDA

ISTANULDA YASAMIS OLAN VE GREK GEMIS

ANSIKLOPEDIK BILGISI GEREK YA SDIGI OSMANLI

IMPARATORLUGU ADLI TARIH ESERI ILE AVRRUPA

DA UN YAPMIS BULUNAN MOLDAVYA PRENSI

DMITRI KANTEMIR IN YEMIDEN INSA ETTIRDIGI

SARAY BUZUNUYORDU.

Translated, this means, DMITRI KANTEMIR, PRINCE OF MOLDAVIA LIVED AND STUDIED HERE FROM 1688-1710.

"Pat, this confirms that this is the palace of your friend's ancestor, Dmitri Kantemir and his wife Cassandra Cantacuzenes. The Cantacuzenes were descendants of Byzantine emperor John Cantacuzene."

"Really, Ferit? I need to take pictures of the ruins and of the plaque for Ella. Let me wipe the plaque again so the writing is visible. I can't believe we have actually found what we have been searching for. Ella will be so surprised," she replied.

Pat took her scarf to wipe away the remaining dirt, only gentler, aware of its significance. As she continued to clean the sign, a feeling of warmth overtook her body. "Is that a lute I hear?" Pat said to no one in particular. She could almost feel Dmitri's presence as if it was 1710.

Without warning, the blue trimmed, white double doors on the upper level of the palace burst open. Prince Dmitri Kantemir stood in the doorway, holding his musical instrument, the tanbur in his hand. He walked briskly through the unscathed palace hallways and down the gold leafed marble staircase that would take him to the bottom of the grand entrance hall with its white matching marble floors.

Dmitiri was a skillful musician of the tanbur. He easily learned the traditions and theory of Ottoman music when he first arrived in Istanbul, as he had been educated in classical music by Greek musicians while still in Moldavia. During his time in Istanbul he became captivated by the tanbur, a long necked Turkish lute. The lute, a pear-shaped object, was made almost entirely of wood and played with a plectrum. Studying the art of the tanbur with respected Greek music teachers, Prince Dmitri learned the secrets of Turkish music. His Ottoman repertoire grew and soon his talent for playing and composing Turkish music became widely known. His command of historical Ottoman repertoire and theory inspired him to compose Ottoman tunes that at times mingled with European harmonic melody. He became a brilliant tanburi player and developed a reputation as the most celebrated musician under Sultan Ahmed III. His compositions gave great glamour to oriental music and as a result, successful Turkish melodies were composed. The Turkish people delighted in his musical talents, for Kantemiroglu had become known as the greatest composer of classical Turkish music. His profound knowledge made it possible for him to create elaborate note markings that helped put works of Turkish composers into note format. He gave private lessons to promote the use of these formats enabling composers to no longer rely on memory.

Originally, Dmitri's palace in the Fener district was the unfinished palace of Prince Serban Cantacuzenes. It was given as a dowry when Serban's daughter Cassandra married Dmitri. The palace was located on the left bank of the Golden Horn and was close to the Fethiye Serefi Mosque. Dmitri wanted to complete the palace for his family, so he took it upon himself to personally draft the designs. He added elements of Oriental architecture in the Byzantine style to the beautiful stone building. A large park and garden in the rear enhanced the estate. The palace was the architecture pearl of Istanbul and cost over $34,000 in gold. It was the envy of many affluent residents. Some even turned to the Sultan in an attempt to halt construction of the magnificent palace and they succeeded, but only temporarily. Prince Dmitri had many contacts in the Ottoman court. With the intercessions of the Grand Vizer Ali Pasa, Dmitri was able to resume the project completing it in 1703.

Many friends and dignitaries were welcomed at the new home and Prince Dmitri became well known for his hospitality. It became the gathering place for the elite, representing musical, scientific, and cultural aspects of Ottoman life. Prominent families, aristocrats, ambassadors, and Grand Vizers of the Ottoman court were all guests at the hospitable prince's home. Top intellectuals such as Saadi Efendi, a researcher and expert of Islam, Raami Mehmed Pasa, a talented poet, musician Levna Celebi, a renowned saz player, and Koran interpreter Nefioglu all frequented Dmitri's palace. International diplomats visited the estate. Dmitri developed friendships with the French and Russian ambassadors. With Ambassador Peter Tolstoy, he discussed the future of the Christian nations in the Balkans. He spoke several languages, Latin, Turkish, Arabic, Moldavian, Greek and Russian with his guests. The Sultan was so impressed with his bi-lingual skills, that he would take delight in asking the prince to translate even when the occasion did not call for it. (The Turkish government would later restore Dmitri's Istanbul Palace in 2007 in a joint program with the European Union and Fatih Municipality as a Social Learning Center & Museum).

It seemed as if only yesterday that the prince first arrived from Moldavia. His father Constantine Cantemir, ruler of Moldavia sent him to Istanbul as a guarantee of the loyalty of Moldavia to the Ottoman Empire. Since Moldavia was governed by the Ottoman Empire, his father wanted to secure the family's position in Moldavia. His son's presence in Istanbul would ensure a harmonious relationship between the two countries.

Upon arrival in the country, Prince Dmitri quickly embraced his new life, immersing in diverse activities. He developed a sincere interest in learning all aspects of Ottoman culture. The Ottoman Court, a place of dangerous intrigues was controlled by powerful members of the Imperial Harem and later by a sequence of Grand Vizers. His friendships with the Sultans and Vizers enabled him to draw practical insight and understanding from observations within the court. He acquired a diversity of creative ideas towards philosophy, and science.

The cosmopolitan aura of the city was the perfect setting to expand his intellectual and artistic creativity. He had an unusual talent for philosophy and music and Istanbul suited him in this self-imposed exile. He studied at the Ecumenical Greek Patriarchate in Fener, becoming acquainted with the theory of natural sciences that influenced his historical thinking. Dmitri studied oriental languages too. He also learned about Ottoman history with theologian Nefioglu and astronomer Esaad Efendi. He took note of events, customs of his new life and studied rare books. He learned useful diplomatic skills, all this, while supervising the building of his new palace in Fener.

During this time in Fener, Prince Dmitri was constantly devising political schemes to obtain the Moldavian throne and crush his enemies. He wrote *Istoria Ieroflific* in 1705, a novel describing the feuds between two families, the Cantemirs of Moldavia and the Brancovans of Wallachia. He used animals and birds to describe the feuds between the two ruling families and their connection to the Ottoman Court.

Prince Dmitri had been appointed to rule his native Moldavia. He would be leaving Istanbul, his home for the last 22 years. He had only left once during that time to marry Princess Cassandra Cantacuzenes of Wallachia, the adjacent kingdom to Moldavia. The Prince knew once he left Istanbul again, he would never see Sultan Ahmed III again. They had known each other for many years and had much in common. They both were the same age and shared the same cultural interests. The Sultan was a patron of literature and art and he enjoyed entertaining as did the Prince, who learned the skill of socializing from observing the Sultan. As a result, Prince Dmitri acquired many friends in Turkish and Tatar diplomatic circles, inviting them to his palace for wine and conversation.

He knew one day the Turks would trust him enough to let him assume rule in Moldavia. That day had arrived. He would be leaving soon to resume his title as the ruler of Moldavia. All the wisdom he had acquired during his many years in the shadows of the Ottoman Court would prove to his advantage. He arrived in Istanbul when he was 15 years old. He was now 37 years old, having spent most of his entire life among the Ottoman Court.

Prince Dmitri looked splendid on this important occasion. He was dressed in his finest, resembling a western knight in an orange buttoned down long jacket. He wore a ceremonial Ottoman turban over his black European wig. He wanted to make a good impression on the Sultan, for tonight would be a bittersweet moment for them both. He was invited to play one final time for Sultan Ahmed III at Topkapi Palace before his departure from Istanbul to govern his native Moldavia.

A special piece was composed for the Sultan on this occasion. Prince Dmitri would personally play the beautiful, wistful *"Saz Semai"* in *'Makam Neva.'* The Sultan would not be disappointed!

Prince Dmitri's brilliant farewell performance for the Sultan foreshadowed his future Moldavian and Russia life. Generations later, it would parallel the life of a descendant, who with the same passion and determination would cross the barriers of time to revive the family history, reclaim her royal heritage and discover her long lost sister in the process.

Three hundred years later, I would be that descendant.

About the Author

Eleonora Borisovna Kantemir is the direct descendant of Prince Dmitri Kantemir, Prince of Moldavia, Prince of the Russian Empire, Prince of the Holy Roman Empire, and Imperial Chancellor to Peter the Great.

Her family's refugee status in the United States compelled her father to stimulate multi-culture awareness, particularly of his time in Russia. Along the way, she became aware of her heritage and the hunt for her father by the Soviets. In the process she found her older sister whom she had never met.

After growing up in Connecticut, and working as a flight attendant out of Iceland and New York, Eleonora eventually settled in Los Angeles, where she began the arduous endeavor of researching her family's past. In time, she visited their former estate, "Tsaritsyno" in Moscow, and found her long lost sister in Azerbaijan, and was informed as to why the Kantemirs had been the target of intelligence operatives.

To learn more about the IRON BLOOD dynasty, or to contact the author, visit:
www.IronBlood-TheDmitriKantemirLegacy.com

Appendix A
Photo Gallery

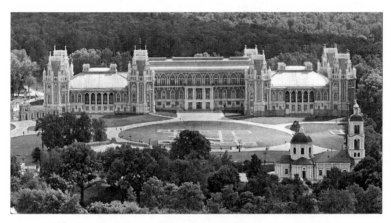

Chornaya Graz (*Tjaritjyno*) Moscow, Russia
Kantemir Estate for Sixty Years
(Sold to Catherine the Great in 1777)

Princess Anastasia Trubetskaya (1700–1755)
(Second Wife of Prince Dmitri Kantemir)

Prince Dmitri Kantemir
1673-1723

Prince of Moldavia — 1693
Prince of the Russian Empire — 1711
Prince of the Holy Roman Empire —
1711 (Title given by Charles VI)

To see more photos of the Kantemir Dynasty visit:
www.IronBlood-TheDmitriKantemirLegacy.com

Bibliography

Cerkova, Zinada, "Maria Kantemir, Princess." Moscow: Astral Transit Books, 2006.

Gaynor, Elizabeth "Russian Houses." New York: Evergreen, (1991): 67-72.

Jones, Maurice Bethell, "Peter Called the Great." New York: Frederick A. Stokes Co. (1936): 353-379.

Massie, Robert, "Peter the Great." New York: Alfred A. Knopf, (1980).

Popescu-Judetz, Eugenia, "A Prince in Two Worlds." New York: The Light Millennium, (2004).

Tvircum, Victor, Ambassador of the Republic of Moldova to Turkey, "Dmitri Kantemir in the History and Culture of the Ottoman Empire." Istanbul: Hurriyet Daily News, (2003).

Wiener, Leo, "Feofan Prokopovich's Funeral Sermon on Peter I. Anthology of Russian Literature from the Earliest Period to the Present Time," (1902): 214-218.

Other Books by
Bettie Young Book Publishers

978-0-9843081-1-8

978-0-9843081-2-5

978-1-936332-22-9

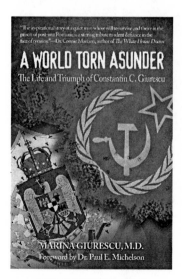

978-1-936332-76-2

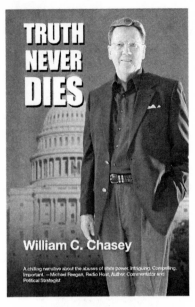

William C. Chasey

A chilling narrative about the abuses of state power. Intriguing. Compelling. Important. —Michael Reagan, Radio Host, Author, Commentator and Political Strategist

978-1-936332-46-5

Melissa McCarty

978-1-936332-69-4

"I base many of my filming decisions on whether or not a story has that extra-special something that I call the goose bump factor. This spellbinding story has it." —Morgan Elliott, Emmy-nominated Producer

The girl who gave her wish away

SHARON BABINEAU

FOREWORD BY CRAIG KIELBURGER, CO-FOUNDER, FREE THE CHILDREN

978-1-936332-96-0

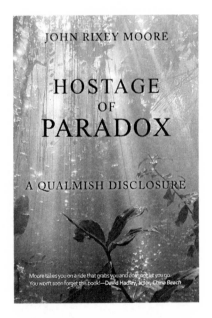

JOHN RIXEY MOORE

HOSTAGE OF PARADOX

A QUALMISH DISCLOSURE

Moore takes you on a ride that grabs you and does not let you go. You won't soon forget this book!—David Hadley, actor, *China Beach*

978-1-936332-37-3

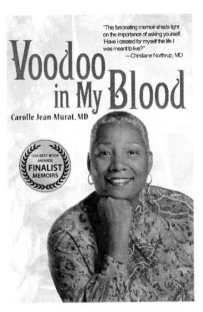

978-1-936332-05-2

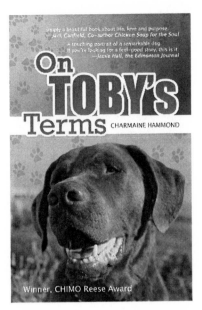

978-1-940784-27-4

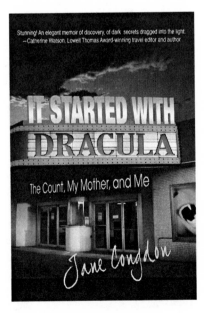

978-1-936332-10-6

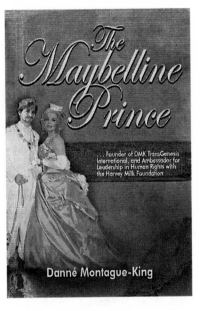

978-1-940784-14-4

978-0-9882848-8-3

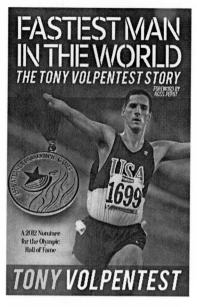

978-1-940784-07-6

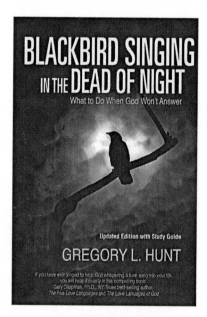

978-1-936332-52-6

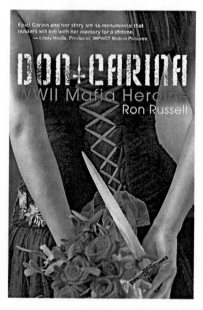

978-0-9843081-9-4